ARNOLD

SCHWARZENEGGER

ARNOLD SCHWARZENEGGER

BROOKS ROBARDS

MAGNA BOOKS

Published by Magna Books
Magna Road
Wigston
Leicester LE8 2ZH

Produced by Bison Books Ltd
Kimbolton House
117A Fulham Rd.
London SW3 6RL

ISBN 1-85422-260-0

Printed in Hong Kong

PICTURE CREDITS

All photos courtesy of Brompton Photo Library except the following:
AP/Wide World Photos: p. 24, 25, 27 (bottom).
© Ron Galella: p. 9 (top), 86 (bottom).
UPI/Bettmann: p. 20-21 (both), 30, 64 (both), 69 (bottom), 77, 86 (top right).

ACKNOWLEDGMENTS

The author and publisher would like to thank the following people who helped with the preparation of this book: Don Longabucco, the designer; Kathy Schneider, the photo researcher; Jean Martin, the editor; and Elizabeth A. McCarthy, the indexer.

Page 1: *Arnold won a dozen world bodybuilding competitions by 1976.*

Page 2: *The role of Conan the Barbarian made Arnold a Hollywood star in the early 1980s.*

Right: *Even before his success in Hollywood, Arnold was an astute businessman, parlaying a mail order business and real estate holdings into a sizeable fortune. In October 1991 he opened Planet Hollywood, a combination restaurant/museum in New York, with Bruce Willis and Sylvester Stallone.*

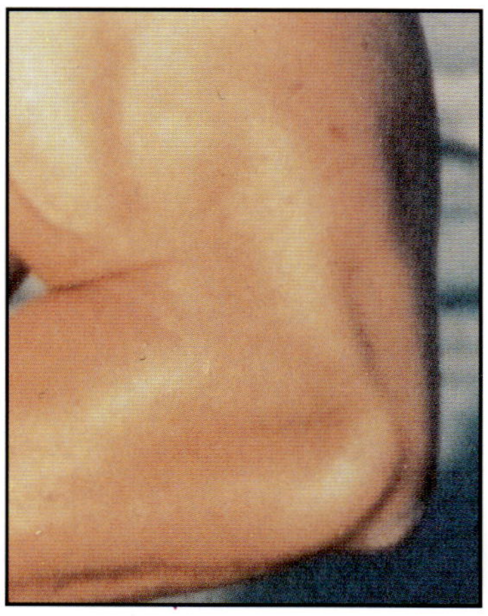

CONTENTS

INTRODUCTION

Arnold Schwarzenegger – legendary muscleman, Hollywood superstar. It was an unlikely scenario for the scrawny Austrian teenager with the gap-toothed smile and an almost unpronounceable name that means "black ploughman." Little about Arnold has turned out to be ordinary.

He climbed his way to fame through bodybuilding, bringing recognition to this obscure sport and winning 13 major titles – more than any bodybuilder in history. His next conquest was Hollywood, where he ignored those who insisted that his overdeveloped body, his almost unintelligible accent and his wooden acting would keep him from the top. He became one of the very few stars who can call their own shots. Along the way, he made millions in real estate, wrote four books on bodybuilding and married into the one American family that comes close to being royalty – the Kennedys. Like the movie characters he plays, he seemed capable of overcoming any obstacle. What is his secret?

The answer lies in the larger-than-life dreams we have as a culture. The myth of the invincible hero is part of our cultural heritage. Homer immortalized the Greek warrior

Opposite: *Arnold spent his early years working to create an ideal body.*

Below: *Arnold enjoys a Cuban Davidoff cigar, an emblem of his success.*

Left: *Arnold poses with one of the creepy cadavers from the set of HBO's* Tales from the Crypt *(1990). He made his debut as a director with an hour-long episode in the series. Called "The Switch," it is the saga of a rich old man who buys himself a new face and body to win the love of a much younger woman. Veteran actor William Hickey, who played the mob chief in* Prizzi's Honor, *starred.*

Achilles. Hercules was the son of the god Zeus and a mortal woman. Samson was one of the judges of Israel. The American folk hero Paul Bunyan was a lumberjack; John Henry, a steel driver. Each of these men was celebrated in his time because of his legendary physical strength.

In our era, physical strength no longer has the same relevance. What, then, explains Arnold Schwarzenegger's appeal?

Arnold recognized the importance of muscles as a symbol. The modern world may not require men to move mountains to survive, but physical strength remains a symbol of manliness. Arnold's obsession as a boy with making his own body into a fortress helped him to understand the need in our culture for masculine superheroes.

Many legendary strong men have a fatal weakness. Achilles could only be killed by a wound to his heel. Samson lost his strength when his hair was cut. In the modern version of the myth, great physical strength, no longer necessary in a world dominated by machines, is its own liability. The progress of Arnold's career makes clear that he had an instinctive understanding of this fact. Recognizing that bodybuilding was really a performance art, he moved on to Hollywood where the only limit on feats of physical strength is the imagination. Because he was an immigrant himself – an outsider – he felt at home in an industry that was built by immigrants. Through hard work and determination, he turned his liabilities into assets. He re-invented the myth of the self-made man.

Arnold has no illusions about his talent as an actor, and popular as his movies are, they may never be considered masterpieces in what has become the greatest storytelling medium of the twentieth century. That does not negate their contribution. The Conans, the Terminators, even the Kindergarten Cops have a great deal to tell us about our dreams – and nightmares – of what it means to be a man today. Arnold's career teaches us that those who master the media and control their public image are the musclemen of the modern world. They are our power brokers.

Above: *Arnold attended the 62nd Oscar ceremony with his wife Maria and his mother-in-law Eunice Kennedy Shriver in 1990. His 1990 movie,* Total Recall, *won an Oscar for Special Effects.*

Right: *Arnold oversees his business operations from an office in Venice, California, near the gym where he works out.*

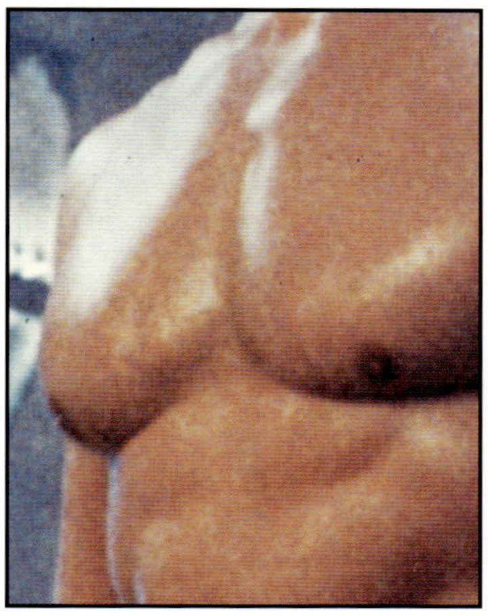

FROM LITTLE ACORNS DO MIGHTY OAK TREES GROW: TO *PUMPING IRON* (1947-77)

The story of Arnold's life – a legend in the making – provides a more fantastic movie script than most of his movies. The Austrian Oak, as he later came to be known, was born on July 30, 1947, in the picturesque village of Thal outside of Graz, an Austrian city near the Hungarian and Yugoslavian borders.

It is hard to conceive of the circumstances in which this international movie star and financial mogul, listed by *Forbes* as one of the ten wealthiest entertainers in America, grew up. His father Gustav was the local police chief. Gustav had married a widow, Aurelia Jadrny, and settled with her in Thal after the war. Their other child, Meinhard, was born a year before Arnold.

Times were hard, and Arnold has described how in

Opposite: *Arnold began bodybuilding at the age of 15. Just a few years later, he won his first competition.*

Below: *Arnold's famous physique often provides the focus in his movies.*

Left: *Arnold wins one of his thirteen major bodybuilding titles. He recounts the story of his climb to victory in the world of bodybuilding in a book he co-authored with Douglas Kent Hall.*

Opposite: *Arnold's success in bodybuilding competition was based on outfoxing opponents, as well as bodily perfection. He was notorious for the pranks he pulled in his early days, including advising one bodybuilder to eat two pounds of ice cream in order to enhance his muscle mass.*

order to gather enough food for the family, his mother went from farm to farm with her two little boys. Meat was a once-a-week item. The family lived on the second floor of a cold, damp, three hundred-year-old house that was the official residence for the chief of police. The Schwarzenegger home had no telephone, no indoor plumbing, no refrigerator.

Although Arnold does not discuss it, his father joined the Nazi party after Austria was annexed by Germany in 1938. Nazi Party membership was not routine in Austria, but support for Hitler in the county of Styria was high during the war. In his autobiography, Arnold describes his father as "always neat, his hair slicked back smooth, his mustache trimmed to a line."

Gustav was a strict disciplinarian, requiring that his sons do sit-ups before breakfast. On weekends, the family enjoyed outings, often to concerts, since Gustav played six instruments and belonged to Graz's police band. Afterwards, the boys were required to write 10-page essays describing the outing. Like a severe schoolmaster, their father would correct errors.

As a small child, Arnold was timid and sickly, a poor second to the blond and handsome brother who was the apple of his mother's and father's eyes. When asked what he wanted to be when he grew up, Arnold answered, "All I want is to go out in the world with a stick, a hat and a monkey."

Whatever his shortcomings, Gustav exerted a major influence in Arnold's life. He spent time with his sons and instilled in Arnold the values of family and discipline. Gustav encouraged his sons to be athletic, and Arnold began playing soccer on a local team at 10. When the coach decided weightlifting might strengthen the boys, Arnold paid his first visit to a bodybuilding gym. "And there it was before me – my life, the answer I'd been seeking. It clicked," he said.

Arnold was fifteen when he decided to be the best bodybuilder in the world. Adopted by the men at the gym, Arnold began training intensively. Nothing else mattered. When his concerned parents restricted his gym visits to three days a week, he put together a gym at home. He stopped going to mass with his family. Girls held little interest.

When he finished schooling at 18, Arnold joined the Austrian Army to fulfill his one-year military obligation. The little boy who had paraded around in his father's uniform loved the regimentation, but he kept his body-building dreams front and center. During basic training he went AWOL in order to compete in – and win – his first bodybuilding contest, the Mr. Europe Junior com-

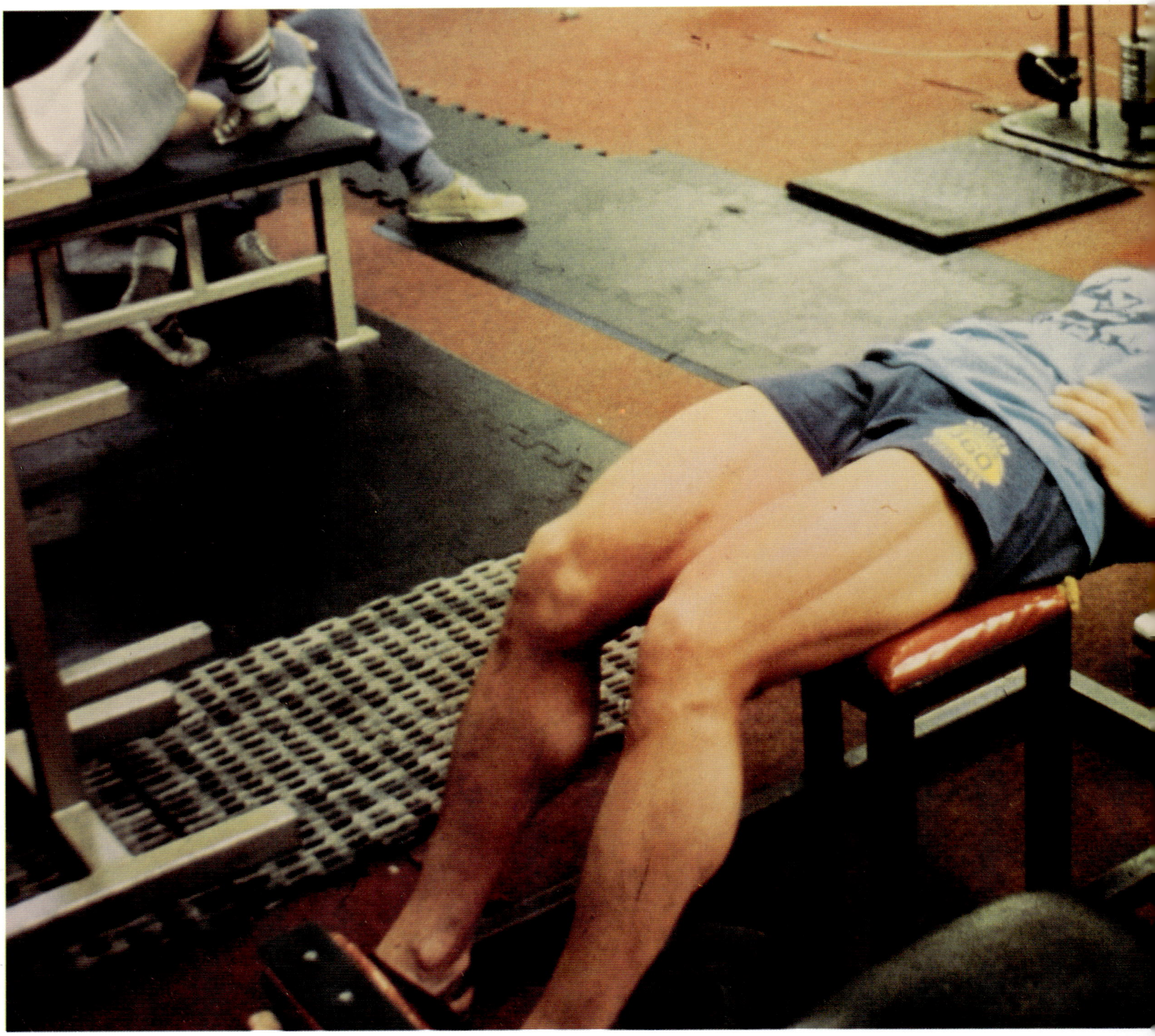

petition in Stuttgart, Germany. He spent seven days in the brig as a result, but the Army quickly recognized his athletic talents, set up a weightlifting gym and put him on a rigorous training program.

Instead of returning home when he finished his military service, Arnold went to work for the owner of a bodybuilding gym in Munich, Germany. Controlling the growth of his muscles and preparing for international competition became an obsession from which neither hardship nor the pleas of his family distracted him. In 1966 Arnold won three German competitions: Mr. Europe, the International Powerlifting Championship and Best Built Man of Europe. The National Amateur Body Builders Association's Mr. Universe title eluded him that year, but just barely. When he won the 1967 Mr. Universe trophy, he told himself, "What is happening right now is the most important moment in your life."

In at least one sense, that moment didn't really come until a year later. After winning a second NABBA Mr. Universe title, Arnold was contacted by American bodybuilding promoter Joe Weider, who asked him to come to the U.S. and compete in the International Federation of Bodybuilders' Mr. Universe competition in Florida. At the last minute and – rumor has it – with the law not far behind him for unspecified offenses, Arnold decided to take up Weider's offer. It was perhaps the most important decision in his life. He arrived in America with a gym bag and little else.

Despite high hopes for taking the U.S. by storm, Arnold came in second in the Miami IFBB Mr. Universe contest. Alone and close to penniless, he said, "I cried all night because of it." The setback was temporary. Determined to take advantage of American expertise in nutrition and drugs, Arnold settled in California and redoubled his training efforts. He has never hidden the fact that he used steroids. The only debate is when he

Above left: *Arnold developed a following at Gold's Gym in the 1970s.*

Top: *Arnold trained six days a week, sometimes fainting from workouts.*

Above: *The budget for Arnold's first film,* Hercules in New York *(1970), was $300,000. It is a spoof of the Hercules muscle movies Arnold watched as a boy in Graz, Austria.*

started and how much he used. Arnold said in recent years that he wished drug testing had begun much sooner in bodybuilding.

In 1970, at the age of 23, Arnold reached the pinnacle of bodybuilding. That year he won the Gold Triangle, the three top competitive events in bodybuilding: Mr. Universe, Mr. World and Mr. Olympia. Before he was finished, Arnold would accumulate five Mr. Universe titles and seven Mr. Olympia crowns, coming out of retirement in 1980 to win a final Mr. Olympia title.

His achievement extends far beyond his titles. Arnold's success won a place of respect for a sport that until then was considered obscure, if not downright comical, and limited to homosexuals. He parlayed the physical fitness craze sweeping his adopted country into respectability for bodybuilding. He also recognized bodybuilding's limitations. With his childhood ambition fulfilled, Arnold set his next goal: Hollywood.

His first film, *Hercules in New York*, produced in 1969 for Italian television and released in 1970, realized his fantasies in a very literal sense. Arnold had seen his first movie at the age of 11 and soon was sneaking in on a regular basis. "My method was to walk in backward when the people were coming out, like I was part of the audience," he explained. He watched John Wayne

Left: *Early in his movie career, Arnold used the pseudonym Arnold Strong. He continued to maintain a heavy workout schedule with split and double split sessions two and three times daily, four or five times a week.*

Opposite: *Elliott Gould and Nina van Pallandt were both featured in* The Long Goodbye *(1973), the first serious movie that Arnold appeared in. Gould made a name for himself in* Bob & Carol & Ted & Alice, *as well as* M*A*S*H. *Van Pallandt appeared in the 1978 film by* Goodbye *director Robert Altman,* A Wedding.

westerns and Johnny Weismuller as Tarzan, but the Hercules movies starring bodybuilders Steve Reeves and Reg Park captured his imagination.

Beginning in 1959 with *Hercules*, the quintessential cloak-and-sandal saga, others in the Italian-made series include *Hercules Unchained, Hercules in Rome, Hercules in the Haunted World, Hercules Against the Moon Men, Hercules Against the Sons of the Sun, Hercules and the Captive Women,* and *Hercules, Samson and Ulysses*. Steve Reeves, at 23 the youngest Mr. Universe until Arnold, was the more popular star in these muscle epics, but Arnold favored Reg Park. After winning second place in the 1966 Mr. Universe contest, he wrote him fan letters and met his idol in 1967 when Park was in London, later visiting him at his home in South Africa.

Arnold's mentor Joe Weider was responsible for his movie debut in *Hercules in New York*. Weider won the part for him by persuading the producer that he was a well-known European actor. Arnold plays the son of Zeus, god of the heavens and weather, and Alcmena, a mortal. Thrown out of Olympus, Hercules lands in New York. His adventures in the metropolis include encounters with beautiful women, wrestling promoters, grizzly bears and gangsters, as well as a thunderbolt-tossing Zeus.

Directed by Arthur Allan Seidelman, the movie is now a laughable late-night TV entry sometimes identified as *Hercules Goes Bananas* or *Hercules – the Movie*. Arnold's voice is dubbed. "I didn't speak English well," Arnold said. "I didn't understand most of what I was saying. I stepped off the boat and starred in a motion picture. It was crazy."

Arnold was billed as "Arnold Strong," a name he has also used on bodybuilding products connected with the mail order business he set up to exploit his success as a bodybuilder. The cast of *Hercules in New York* includes veteran actor Arnold Stang, whose best film is the 1950s Preminger drama *The Man With the Golden Arm*. Also featured are Taina Elg, who appeared in George Cukor's *Les Girls,* and James Karen, who has had roles in *The China Syndrome* and the cult film *Frankenstein Meets the Space Monster*.

After *Hercules in New York*, Arnold's next movie was a significant step up. He has a walk-on in Robert Altman's satire, *The Long Goodbye*. A brilliant director, Altman has made such classics as *M*A*S*H, Nashville,* and *McCabe and Mrs. Miller*.

The Long Goodbye stars *M*A*S*H* alumnus Elliott Gould as private eye Philip Marlowe. The character, created by Raymond Chandler, was made famous by Humphrey Bogart in Howard Hawks's 1946 classic *The Big Sleep*. Altman's *The Long Goodbye* parodies the Hollywood conventions of the hardboiled detective genre, which romanticizes the private eye as a lonely hero battling to bring justice to a corrupt world.

Arnold got his part through actor/acquaintance David Arkin, who plays Harry in the movie. Arkin told Altman, "I've got this big, strong guy for you. His name is Arnold Strong, and he's a weightlifter who just came over from Germany." The director hired Arnold sight unseen. "He was a likeable guy," Altman reportedly said. "He didn't push himself forward at all. And I would never have forecast his success."

Wearing a bright red shirt, Arnold appears toward the end of the movie. He has no speaking lines, and his job is

Above: *In* Stay Hungry *(1976), Arnold worked with Jeff Bridges, appearing as his mentor and guide to the bodybuilding world.*

Opposite: *The benefits of bodybuilding get play in* Stay Hungry. *Arnold helped give bodybuilding a new, improved image.*

to rough up Gould's Marlowe. When gangster Marty Augustine orders everybody to take off their clothes, Arnold strips down to his yellow jockey shorts and flexes his pecs. In the next scene, he gets his hand slapped when he reaches for a bundle of money.

Arnold worked with a rather bizarre collection of actors gathered by Altman. Their real-life stories tend to overlap with their roles in the movie. Former baseball player Jim Bouton plays Marlowe's deceitful best friend, whose apparent suicide launches the action. Nina van Pallandt plays the double-dealing wife of a famous writer. Her main claim to fame at the time was her affair with writer Clifford Irving, who created a scandal by faking a biography of eccentric billionaire Howard Hughes. Marty Rydell, who plays Augustine, is a director as well as an actor.

Although not initially popular, *The Long Goodbye* was re-released and fared better the second time, winning high praise from critics. A corrosive portrait of 1970s decadence, it was shot by one of Hollywood's leading cinematographers, Vilmos Zsigmond, and scored by John Williams.

Arnold was again cast as a muscleman in *Stay Hungry*, released in 1976. This time he had a featured part and played a more sympathetic version of a strongman. Again he worked under a first-rate director. After directing *Five Easy Pieces*, the film that established Jack Nicholson's reputation, Bob Rafelson was known as one of Hollywood's up-and-coming directors.

The plot of *Stay Hungry* concerns an aimless southern rich boy, Craig Blake (Jeff Bridges), who befriends bodybuilder Joe Santo (Arnold). Along the way, Santo teaches Blake about the joys of a simpler, healthier lifestyle and even hands over his ex-girlfriend, Mary Tate Farnsworth (Sally Field). The movie is based on a novel by Charles Gaines, whom Arnold knew through photographer George Butler.

Butler met Arnold at the 1972 Mr. America competi-

tion in Brooklyn, N.Y. He and Gaines were collaborating on a book, *Pumping Iron*, which became the basis for the documentary film that consolidated Arnold's reputation. The book, which was in the works during the period when Arnold was also working on *Stay Hungry*, did not have an easy passage. In his 1990 book *Arnold Schwarzenegger: A Portrait*, Butler describes how his first publisher, Doubleday, rejected the manuscript.

After *Pumping Iron* was brought out by Simon & Schuster in 1974, the *New York Times* refused to review it, saying it was nothing but "fag bait," according to author Butler. An underground success, the book went into fifteen printings. Even a hostile Barbara Walters was disarmed by Arnold during a TV interview for "Today"

when he told her, "I take steroids because they help me an extra five percent. Women take the Pill. They are somewhat similar. I do it under a doctor's supervision." He went on to lecture her about nutrition and physiology. When Lucille Ball heard Arnold wisecrack on "The Merv Griffin Show" that pumping was as good as humping, she hired him for a TV special with Art Carney.

Left: *Sally Fields had a role in* Stay Hungry *that was a departure from her "Flying Nun" persona.*

Above: *In the late 1970s Arnold was a bachelor, appearing here at a New York disco.*

Despite Arnold's credentials in bodybuilding and the juggernaut he had become as a self-publicist, director Rafelson was opposed to using him in *Stay Hungry*. According to Gaines, who collaborated with Rafelson on the script and suggested Arnold for the part of bodybuilder Santo, Rafelson said, "We are not going to use some know-nothing Austrian bodybuilder as a main character in a major motion picture." Rafelson's attitude changed when Gaines brought Arnold over to his house, although the character of Santo was reduced to a supporting role. Calling Jack Nicholson for advice, Rafelson arranged twelve weeks of private lessons with acting teacher Eric Morris.

One casualty of Arnold's burgeoning movie career was his first long-term love relationship. He met English teacher Barbara Outland in 1969, while she was a student working as a waitress in a Santa Monica restaurant. She lived with him, helped him with his studies, his bricklaying and mail order businesses, and even traveled to Europe with him. Although she sup-

ported his documentary on bodybuilding, she drew the line at a career in acting. When Arnold left California for Birmingham, Alabama, where *Stay Hungry* was shot, he and Barbara called it quits, and Arnold's acting career began in earnest.

"I was ripped out of the mentality of being an athlete, where you have to keep the blinders on all the time," Arnold said. "I tapped a new well I had never tapped before. When Sally Field holds you, looks into your eyes and hugs you one last time before she leaves, you believe this, and it shows in your face. You don't have to act, you only have to be yourself."

Rafelson groomed the young actor. "He sent me to all the various television shows and movies that were made in town, so that I could watch and get used to the dialogue, and to what 'action,' 'speed' and all that means," Arnold said. "So I really started educating myself and put the same kind of energy into it as I did with bodybuilding." This meant acting lessons, a dialogue coach, and accent removal classes.

According to an extra on the *Stay Hungry* set, though, Arnold was afraid of acting. After his success in bodybuilding, he felt as if he had gone back to being a child, with everybody telling him what to do. He stood firm in one area. Friends told him to keep the pseudonym Arnold Strong, but he decided to use his real name. "Some day the world is going to know who I am – just by hearing my first name, Arnold," he said. If Schwarzenegger was hard to remember, it would be even harder to forget.

The *Stay Hungry* script called for Arnold to play the fiddle, so Rafelson arranged lessons with bluegrass fiddler Byron Berline, who had recorded with Linda Ronstadt, Bob Dylan and the Rolling Stones. Although Arnold didn't actually have to play the instrument, he learned how to mime so well that oldtimers on the set thought he was really performing.

Berline became a friend, and Arnold offered him a part in the movie. When the 31-year-old musician showed up on the set, though, it turned out Arnold had recommended him for the role of a 70-year-old. Despite the misunderstanding, Berline adapted and scored the movie's country music.

Stay Hungry opened to decidedly mixed reviews. *New York Times* critic Vincent Canby wrote, "*Stay Hungry* has the air of a story repeated by someone who has forgotten the point he set out to make." Stanley Kauffmann of *The New Republic* said, "The picture isn't just unsatisfying, it's a mess – but it's a reasonably important and symptomatic mess." If critics complained about the plot, they almost all loved Arnold. Canby described him as "a nice, honorable young man who appears to be trapped inside a huge, grotesquely muscled body." The *Wall Street Journal* said he radiated "assurance and appeal." *Newsweek* called Arnold "surprisingly good as the muscle man with heart – and pectorals – of gold." The movie uses startling images of him lifting weights in a Batman cape and mask. It closes with a mosaic of bodybuilders arranged on metal fire escapes.

At the 1977 Hollywood Golden Globe awards, Arnold stood on the stage with Jessica Lange, Laurence Olivier, Faye Dunaway and Barbra Streisand to receive the prize for the best male acting debut. The only sour note was the presence of Sylvester Stallone, whose movie *Rocky* won best motion picture. Stallone developed into an intensely disliked rival.

The Arnold publicity machine was gaining full momentum. "I knew I had to use *Pumping Iron* and *Stay Hungry* to go out and do interviews and tell the people that now I'm also getting into acting," Arnold said later. He made a guest appearance as a muscleman on the Karl Malden/Michael Douglas TV series "Streets of San Francisco." Like Burt Reynolds, he posed nude for a *Cosmopolitan* centerfold, although he changed his mind and vetoed appearing in the magazine. He started socializing with actors to get a feel for their mentality.

Without that kind of promotion, neither the book nor the movie *Pumping Iron* would have been funded or released, according to George Butler, who describes himself as "the interpreter between Arnold and the press." To drum up funding for the documentary, Butler put together a promotional film from an exhibition Arnold gave in Holyoke, Massachusetts. After he screened this film

Opposite: *A documentary,* Pumping Iron *(1977) became an underground movie hit for Arnold in his first starring role. It was directed by George Butler and Robert Fiore.*

Above: *Arnold's friend Franco Columbo appeared in* Pumping Iron.

Below: *Lou Ferrigno was Arnold's rival in* Pumping Iron.

Left: *Ballet is part of the training shown in* Pumping Iron.

Opposite: *Shown here posing on the beach at Cannes with a crowd of admirers, Arnold had a knack for self-promotion. One of the surprises in* Pumping Iron *is Arnold's announcement that at age 28 he was retiring from bodybuilding.*

in New York for potential backers, one friend said, "If you ever put this oaf Arnold Schwarzenegger on the screen, you and he will be laughed off 42nd Street."

Part of the publicity drive involved Arnold talking about himself as a piece of classical sculpture, an idea bodybuilding promoter Joe Weider came up with in 1973. In line with the promotion of Arnold as a work of art, Butler decided to put on an artistic exhibition. It was held at the Whitney Museum in New York on February 25, 1976.

By five p.m. that day, fewer than 50 tickets had been sold to "Articulate Muscle – The Body as Art." By 7:30 p.m., though, a crowd of 3000 – more than had ever before attended a single event at the Whitney – were packed into its fourth-floor gallery to see Arnold, Frank Zane and Ed Corney pose. Candice Bergen took pictures of Arnold. Grace Glueck, art critic for the *New York Times*, reviewed the show. Bodybuilding took a giant step forward in credibility, and *Pumping Iron* became a viable movie project.

Working with Robert Fiore, Butler took the movie camera into Gold's Gym in Venice, California, to show Arnold and other bodybuilders preparing for the 1975 Mr. Olympia contest in Pretoria, South Africa. Arnold wins victories over Serge Nubret, Lou Ferrigno, and his best friend Franco Columbo. His childhood idol Reg Park presents the trophy to Arnold. Arnold is portrayed throughout as a star-quality, winning athlete. "I was always dreaming about very powerful people. Dictators and things like that. I was always impressed by people who could be remembered for hundreds of years. Even like Jesus, being remembered for thousands of years," Arnold tells the camera.

His winning 6′ 2″, 210-lb frame is contrasted with that of Lou Ferrigno, who at 6′ 5″ and 265 lbs, seemed likely to dethrone Arnold. Like Arnold, Ferrigno's father was a policeman. Unlike him, Brooklyn-raised Ferrigno trained with the active, even overbearing participation of his father. Ferrigno went on to success as The Incredible Hulk in a movie and TV series, as well as in a variety of muscleman movies.

Pumping Iron had a New York premiere on January 18, 1977, with celebrities Carly Simon, James Taylor, Carroll Baker and Tom Wolfe in attendance. The critics were lavish with praise. *New York* magazine said Arnold "lights up the film like neon every time he comes on-screen. Blond and Germanic, muscular beyond all conceiving, he looks like a walking incarnation of the Mighty Thor, the Marvel Comics superhero."

Although an accomplished self-promoter, Arnold had help for the film from New York P.R. expert Bobby Zarem. He posed for artist Jamie Wyeth and photographer Robert Mapplethorpe, ate at Elaine's restaurant, partied with Andy Warhol, and with Jacqueline Kennedy Onassis and Pat Lawford, who would become his aunts by marriage. Morley Safer did a segment entitled "Pumping Gold" on "60 Minutes." At the 1977 Cannes Film Festival, Arnold appeared on the beach with a bevy of dancers from the Paris nightclub Crazy Horse, and fifty thousand people showed up to watch. Arnold had arrived.

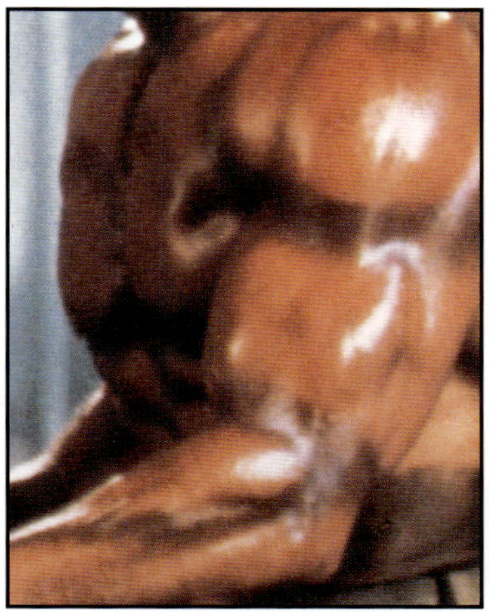

CONAN CONQUERS HOLLYWOOD (1979-84)

The five years following *Pumping Iron's* release were a period of consolidation and transition for Arnold. Since his arrival in California, he had taken courses at Santa Monica City College, West Los Angeles College and UCLA. By combining credits, he earned a degree in business and international economics from the University of Wisconsin.

Romance came into his life again, first with hairdresser Sue Moray, whom he met on the beach in Venice, California, in July 1977, and then with Kennedy clan member Maria Shriver, whom he met at the Robert F. Kennedy Pro-Celebrity Tennis Tournament in Forest Hills, N.Y., in August 1977.

When he was at home in California, Arnold lived with Moray, but it was Maria he courted and ultimately married. The daughter of JFK's sister Eunice and Sargent Shriver, Maria invited her future husband to spend a weekend at the Kennedy family compound in Hyannis Port, Massachusetts. After a year, Moray dropped out of the competition. By then, Maria was well on her way to achieving celebrity in her own right as a network TV journalist.

Arnold had officially retired from bodybuilding competition after the 1975 Mr. Olympia contest on which *Pumping Iron* was based. With the help of author Douglas Kent Hall, he wrote an autobiography, *Arnold: The Education of a Bodybuilder*, published in 1977, which made the top ten of the *New York Times* bestseller list. Arnold, who had already been doing volunteer work in prisons, became active in the Special Olympics, a charitable athletic organization for the mentally handicapped started by Eunice Kennedy Shriver.

Hollywood success came slowly. Arnold's last film in the 1970s was *The Villain*, a western spoof filmed in Tucson, Arizona, that bombed at the box office. Director Hal Needham was a former stuntman who specialized in action comedies and made the Burt Reynolds hits *Smokey and the Bandit* and *Hooper*.

Headliners for *The Villain* were Kirk Douglas and Ann-Margret. Arnold was happy to work with Douglas, the

Opposite: *Arnold's first major Hollywood hit,* Conan the Barbarian *(1982) was based on the Swords and Sorcery tales written by Robert E. Howard.*

Right: *Since the 1970s Arnold has been involved in the Special Olympics, an athletic event designed for the handicapped that was started by his mother-in-law Eunice Kennedy Shriver.*

Left: *Arnold appeared in the 1979 comedy* The Villain *with Kirk Douglas and Ann-Margret. He earned $275,000 for his role as Handsome Stranger.*

Opposite: *In two scenes from* The Villain, *Arnold appears* **(above)** *with comedienne Ruth Buzzi, who starred in TV's "Laugh-In," and* **(below)** *Ann-Margret, who had starred in* Magic *and* The Cheap Detective *the year before.*

star of such macho classics as *Spartacus, Gunfight at the O.K. Corral* and *Paths of Glory*. He told *Time* magazine Douglas was "very muscular and lean and in great shape." Ann-Margret, who won praise for her performance in the 1971 film *Carnal Knowledge*, had worked with such prestigious directors as Tony Richardson, Richard Attenborough and Claude Chabrol.

The Road Runner-like plot of *The Villain* centers on bankrobber Cactus Jack (Douglas). Cactus tries to intercept Ann-Margret's Charming Jones, who is on her way home with the money that will save her father's silver mine from foreclosure. Riding home in the buckboard with Charming is Handsome Stranger (Arnold) who, much to Charming's chagrin, is impervious to her beauty.

Critics complained about outworn camera tricks like split screens and fast motion, as well as bad timing. Janet Maslin of the *New York Times* called Arnold "more of a weight on the movie than even he might be able to lift." Another critic claimed Cactus Jack's horse could act better than Arnold.

Director Needham had praise for Arnold, though, calling him a delight to work with. "He's very funny and is a nice guy," Needham said. "He is professional and eager to learn. He played a straight man to Ann-Margret with all that cleavage. I think he did that very well." Arnold went to the 1979 Cannes Film Festival to promote *The Villain* with Maria in tow.

Despite his lack of movie success, he turned down an offer to play a muscleman in *Sextette*, the 1978 Mae West bomb. When he heard Dino De Laurentiis was planning a new version of the comic book classic Flash Gordon, he met with the Italian producer. He said the meeting lasted exactly one minute and forty seconds.

"I walked in, and I just kept staring at this desk," Arnold said. "It was enormous. Antique. Probably from Italy somewhere. And he was standing behind the desk. And only his shoulders and his head stuck out above it. I just couldn't figure it. So I asked him, 'Why does a little man like you need such a big desk?'"

An irate De Laurentiis said he couldn't use Arnold because of his accent. "What do you mean *I* have an accent? I barely can understand *you*," Arnold said. Luckily for Arnold, De Laurentiis didn't hold a grudge. He eventually signed Arnold for a five-film contract including the two Conan movies that established Arnold as a star.

One area of promotion where Arnold drew the line was commercials. He rejected a $200,000 offer to sell tires and has consistently refused to put his talents to work advertising anybody's products but his own.

Working as a sports commentator for CBS in 1979, he covered the Mr. Olympia contest in Columbus, Ohio, and the Philadelphia Miss Olympia contest in 1980. Initially scheduled to attend the 1980 Mr. Olympia contest in Australia as a TV commentator, Arnold entered the contest himself. Although he had retired from active competition, he was in training for his part as bodybuilder Mickey Hargitay in the TV movie *The Jayne Mansfield Story*. With more than a little grumbling from the other contestants, an undertrained, out-of-shape Arnold won his seventh and final Mr. Olympia title.

Elements of *The Jayne Mansfield Story* had an eery resemblance to Arnold's own life. The subject, blonde bombshell Mansfield, rivalled Marilyn Monroe for the title of most desirable female body in the world and supposedly had an IQ of 162. She married the 1956 NABBA Mr. Universe, Mickey Hargitay, whom she met while he

& MA

Left: *Loni Anderson, who created the role of Jennifer for TV's "WKRP in Cincinnati," starred in Arnold's first TV movie, "The Jayne Mansfield Story," in 1980. Arnold played Mansfield's second husband, bodybuilder Mickey Hargitay.*

Opposite: *For his role in* Conan the Barbarian, *Arnold stripped down to a loincloth and endured a variety of abuses during filming, such as being bitten by a camel and run over by horses.*

was appearing as the beefcake in a Mae West review at the New York Latin Quarter. Mansfield starred in a series of mostly forgettable movies during the 1950s and 1960s, although she also starred in the Broadway hit *Will Success Spoil Rock Hunter*? In contrast to the ultimate outcome of Arnold's career, Mansfield's disintegrated into alcohol abuse and other forms of decadence. She was killed in a grisly automobile accident in which she was decapitated.

Arnold was clearly determined to avoid the pitfalls that dragged down Mansfield. Talking about the prejudice he experienced in Hollywood, Arnold said, "The people in Hollywood had many reasons why I could not make it: my accent, my body, my long name. You just turn the whole thing around. That is what black actors do – including people like Bill Cosby and Eddie Murphy. They've created a certain thing that no one can touch; no one can compete with them. Studios can't do what they did to Marilyn Monroe and Jayne Mansfield and all those girls years ago."

The Jayne Mansfield Story aired October 29, 1980 and starred Loni Anderson, who would later marry Burt Reynolds. Gossip from the set said that one of her love scenes with Arnold got so steamy Anderson called out "cut" before director Dick Lowry could. Arnold blushed, and Anderson told him, "Thank you. If I ever get divorced, I'll look you up."

Conan the Barbarian, the movie with which Arnold made his mark on Hollywood, was based on the mythical world created by an obscure writer from Texas named Robert E. Howard. Howard developed the character of Conan in 1934 for the pulp magazine *Weird*

Opposite: *Cast as Conan's love interest was dancer Sandahl Bergman. Arnold and Bergman took to calling each other Hansel and Gretel during shooting.*

Right: *Arnold trained arduously for the sword fighting in* Conan. *Director John Milius insisted on authentic weapons rather than permitting lighter-weight replicas.*

Tales. His work was fashioned after the Pellucidar stories written in the 1920s by Edgar Rice Burroughs, creator of Tarzan. Blood, gore and vengeance provide the main ingredients for the muscular Cimmerian's adventures.

An only child, Howard wrote 21 Conan stories by 1936, when he shot himself at 30 after learning that his mother was dying. The stories, which were mostly published posthumously, were repackaged as paperbacks in the mid-1960s. Also adapted as comics, they helped establish the fantasy subgenre known as S & S, or Swords and Sorcery.

Businessman Edward J. Pressman bought the movie rights to Conan. Pressman was in favor of casting Arnold as the barbarian superhero, but when the project got underway, the producer was Dino De Laurentiis, who favored a big-name actor. Calling Arnold a "Nazi," he refused even to consider him.

Director John Milius landed the part for Arnold. He told De Laurentiis Arnold was the world's most perfectly built man. De Laurentiis relented, and Arnold got the part. "I've never been wrong yet with my instincts," Arnold said, "and they tell me this is going to be a really big film, a whole new phenomenon. I don't care what it takes; I don't care if I have to take one year out of my life and be an animal. I know this film is going to be unbelievable for me."

Arnold said of his director, "If I have to do films the

Left: *As the hero of* Conan the Barbarian, *Arnold is enslaved and acquires his magnificent physique through hard labor. His prowess as a gladiator á la* Spartacus *ultimately persuades his captor to set him free.*

Opposite top: *Conan acquires the sword that had belonged to his father, murdered by the villain Thulsa Doom.*

Opposite bottom: *Conan encounters a magical witch, played by Cassandra Gaviola.*

rest of my life with John Milius directing, I will be very, very happy." One of the California film-school-trained directors described as the "movie brat" generation, which also includes Steven Spielberg and Paul Schrader, Milius is a screenwriter as well as a director. He is also a genuine eccentric.

Once describing himself as a "Zen Fascist," saying "I'm so far to the right I'm probably an anarchist," Milius developed a media reputation as a gun-slinging reactionary. One journalist who visited him at his Bel Air home reported he was shown Milius's personal armory and told, "My family will be one of the last to go if it comes to a fight." Members of his production company, named A-Team after the Green Beret designation, were rumored to click their heels and give mock Nazi salutes.

Milius's movie credentials are impressive, if violence-oriented. He co-wrote *Apocalypse Now* and *Jeremiah Johnson* and did the script for *The Life and Times of Judge Roy Bean*. Although uncredited, he helped write Clint Eastwood's *Dirty Harry* and is responsible for the original script of the sequel *Magnum Force*. The films he directed, including *Dillinger, The Wind and the Lion, Big Wednesday, Red Dawn* and *Farewell to the King*, met with mixed reviews. He wrote the script for *Conan* with Oliver Stone, who went on to become a celebrated director in his own right.

"He's not a natural," Milius said of Arnold. "He'll learn, and he'll improve, but he's not an actor. It's [acting is] demeaning to a man. From the point of view of someone who is displaying himself, it is not pure. It's not an occupation for a superhero."

Cast opposite Arnold was distinguished actor James Earl Jones, best known at the time as the voice of Darth Vader in *Star Wars*, and Max Von Sydow, one of the regulars in Ingmar Bergman's films. Dancer Sandahl Bergman, whose Hollywood break came in *All That Jazz*, provides the love interest.

Budgeted at $19 million, *Conan the Barbarian* was filmed in Spain. The early scenes were shot in Segovia in subzero temperatures, while later sections were filmed in Almeria, which was scorching and mosquito-ridden. Arnold arrived on location a month before shooting started in order to prepare, and did all his own stunts.

Milius took Arnold skeet- and trapshooting, all the while discussing Conan's character. According to Arnold, Milius "would watch my facial expressions and

Opposite: *Conan forms a partnership with Valeria (Sandahl Bergman) to avenge his parents' deaths and end a snake cult described by one critic as "something like the latest Beverly Hills fad."*

Right: *Max von Sydow, who starred in numerous films by Swedish director Ingmar Bergman, plays King Osric.*

Below: *Conan does battle with one of Thulsa Doom's minions.*

Opposite top: *Valerie Quennessen plays Princess Yasimina, King Osric's daughter, whom Conan rescues from the snake cult.*

Opposite bottom: *Although Valeria (Sandahl Bergman) succeeds in rescuing Conan more than once, she ends up losing her own life.*

Right: *Renowned actor James Earl Jones plays the evil Thulsa Doom, who murders Conan's parents at the beginning of the film and heads the snake cult that Conan ultimately destroys.*

memorize them." Then on the set, Milius would call for particular expressions from Arnold.

The Milius credo was, "Pain is only temporary, but the film is going to be permanent." Authenticity was especially important to Milius. "If you're attacked by a vulture, he wants a real vulture," Arnold said. "If you fight with broadswords, he wants real swords that weigh ten pounds."

A scene involving wolves left Arnold with a cut that required stitches. "I worked seven days straight every morning with dogs – being attacked by five or ten different dogs – just to get rid of the fear. When it came time for that scene, which was the first one we shot, the animals escaped too early and I was not all the way up on the rocks yet. So they pulled me down and I fell ten feet on my back. All of a sudden I had on top of me four of those animals. John came over and said, 'Well, now you know what the film is going to be like.'"

Arnold admitted that the love scenes were difficult. "Before, nobody had asked us whether we wanted something to drink between takes, and now every other minute here are five guys saying, 'Arnold, do you want some orange juice?' while they're looking up and down. That was kind of uncomfortable and laughter was the only way we could get through it." Arnold and Sandahl took to calling each other Hansel and Gretel.

After a quote from Nietzsche, "That which does not kill you will make you strong," the movie opens with the Wizard of the Mounds reciting to a young Conan in stentorian tones from *The Nemedian Chronicles*.

What follows is a tale of unrelenting violence. Young Conan's parents are murdered by Thulsa Doom (James Earl Jones) and Conan is enslaved, transformed into a young giant through his labors on the Wheel of Pain. Trained as a gladiator, he is set free by his owner Red Hair (Luis Barboo) and sets out to seek revenge.

Opposite: *Petite Olivia D'Abo plays the princess whom Conan sets out to rescue in the Conan sequel,* Conan the Destroyer *(1984). D'Abo has also appeared in* Mission Kill, Into the Fire, *and* Beyond the Stars.

Right: *Former basketball star Wilt Chamberlain plays Bombaata in* Conan the Destroyer. *As captain of Queen Taramis's elite guard, his secret mission is to kill Conan.*

After a fiery encounter with a witch (Cassandra Gaviola), Conan teams up with Subotai (Gerry Lopez), meets a wizard (Mako), and then joins forces with Valeria (Bergman) to scale a snake tower. King Osric (Max Von Sydow) commissions the three thieves to rescue his daughter (Valerie Quennessen). Before the mission is accomplished, Conan has been crucified on the Tree of Woe and rescued by Subotai and Valeria. Valeria is killed in the escape with the Princess, but Conan beheads Thulsa Doom and puts an end to the snake cult.

Released on May 14, 1982, *Conan the Barbarian* had a ready-made audience of Howard addicts and grossed $9.6 million in its first weekend. Critics were decidedly mixed in their reactions. *Rolling Stone* complained, "As a director, Milius himself is a bit of a barbaric thief, borrowing liberally from every possible epic movie master from Eisenstein to Peckinpah." But the reviewer found Arnold "rather likeable. He's at ease with his body, and his ultra-blank deadpan provides an amusing comment on all the sound and the fury exploding around him."

Vincent Canby in the *New York Times* felt Arnold lacked grace. "This physical awkwardness eventually becomes the rhythm of the movie itself, as Conan faces one plastic peril and laboratory special effect after another." *Film Comment* found Arnold most effective in repose, but concluded, "He still cannot quite negotiate Conan's 'gigantic melancholies' – his eyes aren't quite as sullen as Howard described them and as the various illustrators have emblematically depicted – but the physique is role-perfect, even if here it's more refined and less flaunted than before." The *Los Angeles Herald Examiner* said Arnold was "about as emotive as a treetrunk."

Conan the Barbarian didn't need the critics' seal of approval; it went on to gross over $100 million worldwide. Sandahl Bergman performed "Eye of the Tiger" with the Temptations at the 1983 Academy Awards ceremony. The next year, Arnold gave out the Scientific and Technical Awards with Joan Collins. The release of a sequel, *Conan the Destroyer*, was soon to follow.

Shooting began on location in Samalayuca, Mexico, in November 1983. This time, the director was Richard Fleischer, a mainstream Hollywood journeyman in contrast to Milius. His film credits stretched back to the 1949 film noir *Follow Me Quietly*, and he is probably best known for the 1954 Disney science fiction epic *20,000 Leagues Under the Sea*. He also was responsible for a range of genre films including *The Vikings, Barabbas, Fantastic Voyage, The Boston Strangler, Tora! Tora! Tora!*, and *The New Centurions*.

When Arnold invited Fleischer over to his house for a sword demonstration with Japanese master Yamasaki, Fleischer applauded but had a request that caught Arnold offguard: "Could you put on more muscles?" Arnold dutifully gained an extra ten pounds.

Sharing the marquee with Arnold in *Conan the Destroyer* were pop singer Grace Jones (Zula) and basketball great Wilt "The Stilt" Chamberlain (Bombaata). Sarah Douglas, who appeared in *Superman* and *Superman II*, played the villainess Queen Taramis, while 15-year-old Olivia D'Abo played Princess Jehenna.

Although *Conan the Destroyer* begins with the same heavyhanded voiceover as the original, Stanley Mann's screenplay has a lighter touch. Conan is more apt to make jokes and becomes the butt of a few. The tone is set in the first scene, when he wisecracks to his milquetoast sidekick Malak (Tracey Walter) that maybe the armored riders galloping up really "want to capture us and torture us to death."

In fact, it's evil Queen Taramis, who offers to bring Conan's lost love Valeria back from the dead if he will

help her niece Princess Jehenna retrieve a magic key and a jewelled horn. What Taramis doesn't tell Conan is that she has ordered her aide Bombaata to kill him once the mission is accomplished. Then she plans to sacrifice Jehenna to the god Dagoth, who will come alive when the jewelled horn is reset in his brow.

Jack Cardiff's cinematography is more lyrical than Duke Callaghan's was in *Conan the Barbarian*, and the emphasis in *Conan the Destroyer* shifts from bleak, revenge-ridden landscapes to enchanted forests and castles. In addition to being better humored, Conan becomes less the loner in the sequel.

Conan the Barbarian is a pessimistic paean to the power of the sword, while *Conan the Destroyer* is more relaxed and takes itself much less seriously. In the sequel, Conan's machismo is not so extreme that he can't give Princess Jehenna lessons in sword fighting and enjoy the platonic companionship of his female counterpart, wild-eyed Zula.

Some of the critics liked *Conan the Destroyer* a little better than the original. As with *Conan the Barbarian*, though, the voice of the critics was lost in a stampede to the box office. *Conan the Destroyer* grossed over $100 million worldwide. Arnold had conquered Hollywood.

Opposite top: *In the Chamber of Mirrors, Conan is locked in a struggle to the death with the evil wizard Thoth-Amon , played by Pat Roach.*

Opposite bottom: *Conan agrees to rescue Princess Jehenna (Olivia D'Abo) in exchange for bringing his lost love Valeria back to life.*

Right and below: *As Amazon-like Zula, singer Grace Jones holds her own in combat. A year later Jones appeared in the James Bond movie,* A View to a Kill.

Above: *The rescue of Princess Jehenna involves Conan's betrayal by Bombaata.*

Right: *Once the magic horn is placed on the head of Dagoth, the god comes to life. Conan slays him, Princess Jehenna accedes to Shatizar's throne, and Conan leaves to find his own kingdom.*

Opposite: *A box-office success,* Conan the Destroyer *was the first film in which Arnold's distinct brand of tongue-in-cheek humor shines through.*

"I'LL BE BACK!": *THE TERMINATOR* TO *COMMANDO* (1984-85)

The appeal Arnold established in his early films was that of a macho superhero who showed off his superb physique by wearing as few clothes as possible. The camera loved both his muscles and the craggy contours of his face. His tough-man signature was stony silence. In the set piece from *Conan the Barbarian*, uttered in response to the question, what is best in life, Conan answers, "To crush your enemies, see them driven before you and to hear the lamentations of the women." The words are delivered in a heavy accent reminiscent of Dr. Strangelove, which was mimicked by fans, on talk shows and by Albert Brooks in *Broadcast News*.

If Arnold had allowed himself to continue making Conan clones, his career might have stalled. Instead he moved away from the rather specialized fantasies of swords and sorcery into the kind of violent realism that could grab the mainstream movie audience.

On the surface, *The Terminator* looked like just another run-of-the-mill B-movie sci-fi project. Although intriguing, the concept was hardly original, mixing elements of sci-fi writer Philip K. Dick's stories "Third Variety" and "Claw" with themes from *Blade Runner, Alien* and *2001: A Space Odyssey*. A killer cyborg – half man, half machine – is sent back from the future to track

Opposite: *Arnold shifted to sci-fi in* The Terminator *(1984).*

Below: The Terminator *was Arnold's first critical success.*

Below right: *Award-winning special effects designer Stan Winston included a sequence where Arnold removes his eye.*

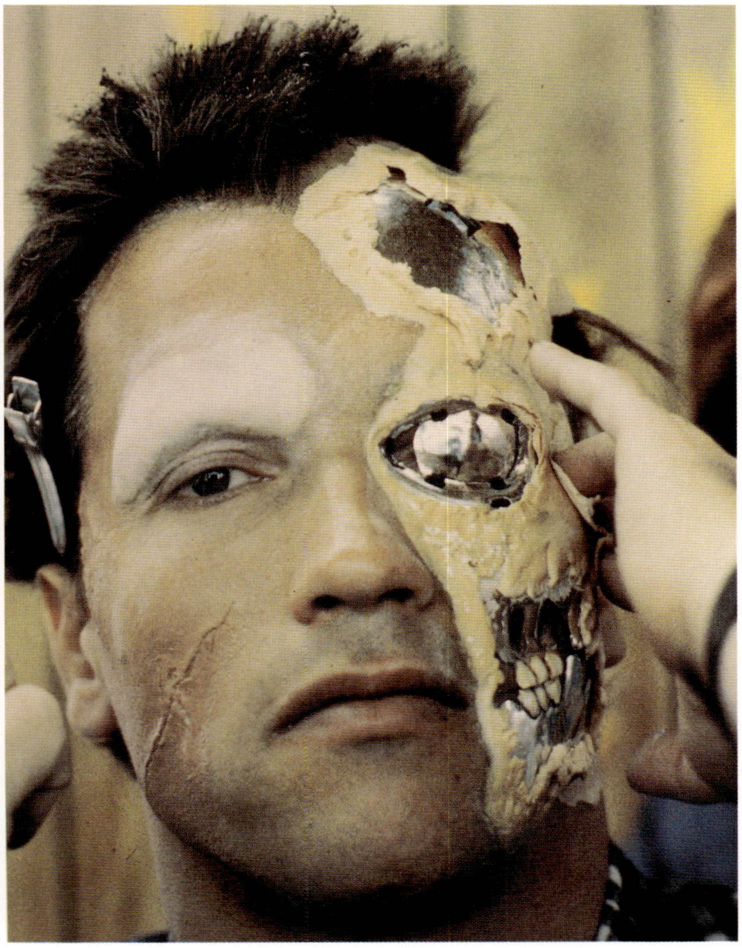

Above: *Arnold's co-stars were Linda Hamilton and Michael Biehn.*

Below: *The Terminator first confronts his quarry at Tech Noir.*

down and kill Sarah Connor, the young woman destined to conceive and bear a son who will save the world from the machines that have taken over in the twenty-first century.

Initially Arnold tried out for the part of Kyle Reese, the young guerrilla who comes back from the future to rescue Sarah Connor and her future son. Instead, Arnold found irresistible the role of the Terminator, the cyborg killer. The movie's laser guns and other sci-fi technology appealed to him, along with the Uzi submachine gun that was guarded by two FBI agents while it was on the set. Filming began on March 19, 1984.

Director James Cameron was a recent graduate of the Roger Corman school of low-budget moviemaking. After one less-than-promising directorial credit – *Piranha II: The Spawning* – Cameron developed the Terminator concept, co-wrote the script with his then-wife, producer Gale Anne Hurd, and set about directing the movie that would catapult both them and Arnold to the top of the box office.

Starring with Arnold are Linda Hamilton (Sarah Connor) and Michael Biehn (Kyle Reese). Hamilton is probably best known for her television portrayal of Katherine in *Beauty and the Beast*. Biehn, the veteran of four forgettable earlier movies, went on to star in Cameron's next two movies, *Aliens* and *The Abyss*. Also featured in *The Terminator* is Paul Winfield (Traxler), who starred in *Conrack* and *Sounder*.

As with *Conan the Destroyer*, part of the effectiveness of *The Terminator* is the movie's exaggerations and tongue-in-cheek tone. Arnold deserves some of the credit. Cameron explained that he had envisioned

Right: *The plot of* The Terminator *concerns a killer cyborg (Arnold) sent back from the future to kill Sarah Connor (Linda Hamilton), who is destined to have a son who will battle and defeat the machines who have taken over the world in the twenty-first century. Kyle Reese (Michael Biehn) is also returned from the future, to defend Sarah and his future son.*

someone more anonymous and saturnine for the role. "With Arnold," he said, "the film took on a larger-than-life sheen. I just found myself on the set doing things I didn't think I would do – scenes that were supposed to be purely horrific that just couldn't be, because they were now too flamboyant."

Although Arnold has only 14 lines of dialogue, what he says is memorable. "I'll be back" became the catch phrase for 1984 and has reappeared in subsequent Arnold films. Arnold said Cameron "liked the idea of my saying those lines like a machine – very slow and very clear and very dead. As time went on, we realized the people really enjoyed the humorous stuff more than the action, because in those test cards, their favorite scene was always a humorous one."

Cameron concentrated on the development of plot and character. He said he and Hurd had "set out to make a movie that would function on a couple of levels: as a linear action piece that a 12-year-old would think was the most *rad* picture he'd ever seen, and as science fiction that a 45-year-old Stanford English prof would think had some sort of socio-political significance between the lines – although obviously it doesn't attempt to be that primarily."

The director focused on the image of the robot. Cameron had in mind an indestructible machine – an endo-skeletal design – something that had never been filmed before. He believes everyone has a little of the Terminator in them. "In our private fantasy world we'd all like to be able to walk in and shoot somebody we don't like, or to kick a door in instead of unlocking it; to be immune, and just to have our own way every minute," he said. "It's a dark, cathartic fantasy."

Cameron defends the movie's violence by saying, "It doesn't have the implication of going out and making the world better with a .44 Magnum." Arnold adds, "It's easy to blame a movie rather than yourself. I watched violent movies all my life and it had no influence on me. Something on the screen doesn't turn a person into a killer unless there's something already wrong with him."

The Terminator was released toward the end of 1984 and became the number one movie in the U.S. for six weeks, grossing over $100 million worldwide. Arnold was named International Star of the Year, and *Time* magazine listed the movie among its ten best. "*The Terminator* automatically doubled my price," Arnold said. A studio executive called him up after seeing the movie and said, "I can't believe it. I only saw you a few seconds

Left: *Director James Cameron points out that the final, robotic version of the Terminator is prepared for by earlier scenes where he repairs himself. The robot even matches Arnold's lumbering gait.*

Opposite: *Arnold returned to the Hyperborean Age in* Red Sonja *(1985). The film did not, however, win the box office success of either* Conan the Barbarian *or* The Terminator.

Overleaf: *Arnold was a somewhat reluctant participant in his final S & S film,* Red Sonja. *He was rumored to have had a romance with co-star Brigitte Nielsen.*

without your clothes on, and they all went for it." Ironically, *The Terminator* was the first film where Arnold appears in the buff. Now he has a nudity clause in his contracts.

Like it or not, the critics had to start taking Arnold seriously. One called his role the greatest horror performance since Boris Karloff. *Cosmopolitan* said, "Sans dialogue, he managed to bring humor, pathos, and life to his role as a robot."

In the *New York Times*, Janet Maslin grudgingly declared, "Arnold Schwarzenegger is about as well-suited to movie acting as he would be to ballet, but his presence in *The Terminator* is not a deterrent." Richard Corliss of *Time* said, "Scratch a critic and you'll get an admission that Schwarzenegger's films have the quality of ferocity. There is something in Arnold that sparks the pinwheeling imaginations of action directors."

The Terminator was the first Arnold movie that film scholars took a second look at. Some saw it as an allegory about changing roles in the family. Others argued over whether the prominence given to Sarah Connor gave it a feminist spin, although the consensus was that the message is the same old, powerfully masculine one dressed up in more modern clothes.

Film Comment called Arnold "a last-gasp parody of post-feminist machismo." "Never viable as a model for masculinity in the eighties, he semi-cleverly opted to be its mockery," Gavin Smith concluded. Director Cameron had another interpretation. "I don't think anybody sees him in a sexual way in the film. They see him almost from the beginning as this implacable, sexless, emotionless machine – in the form of a man, which is scary, because he's a perfect male figure."

"I have a love interest in every one of my films – a gun," Arnold joked. "As long as the woman is a token, I won't do the movie. It has to be like *The Terminator*, where the woman is the main character – where the story revolves around her. Then it is perfect. Then she comes out the hero."

Arnold returned to the Hyperborean Age for his next

Right: *Arnold's co-star Brigitte Nielsen made her acting debut in* Red Sonja. *She later appeared in* Rocky IV, Cobra, Beverly Hills Cop II, Bye Bye Baby *and* Domino.

Opposite top: *As Kalidor, Arnold challenges Red Sonja to a duel that will determine who is the best warrior.*

Opposite bottom: *Also appearing with Arnold in* Red Sonja *were veteran actor Paul Smith as Falkon and Ernie Reyes Jr. as Prince Tarn.*

film. *Red Sonja* showcases pulp author Robert E. Howard's female counterpart to Conan, and producer De Laurentiis spent a year looking for the right actress to play the part. He found her in the form of Danish fashion model Brigitte Nielsen. A statuesque 5-feet 11-inches, Brigitte had a reputation for tempestuousness and had no acting experience.

The script by Clive Exton and George MacDonald Fraser concentrates on the exploits of the flame-haired Amazon (Nielsen) as she avenges her family's death at the hands of Queen Gedren (Sandahl Bergman, who played Arnold's love interest in *Conan the Barbarian*). The evil queen has also stolen a talisman that controls the world. Sonja teams up with a young Prince (Ernie Reyes Jr.) and his factotum (Paul Smith).

As the warrior Kalidor, Arnold plays second fiddle to Sonja. He was not happy with the role. The movie is essentially female S & S, with Sonja rejecting Kalidor's offers of help and telling him, "No man may have me unless he's beaten me in a fair fight." Although Arnold tried to withdraw from the project, his contractual commitment to De Laurentiis made that impossible.

Shooting for the film began in the Pontini Studios in Rome on September 24, 1984, with Richard Fleischer, who had shepherded *Conan the Destroyer* to box office success, in charge. By November Arnold was rumored to be involved romantically with Nielsen. They flew to Vienna together early in December and visited one of Arnold's bodybuilding friends. Then the two travelled to Munich, and on to a ski resort outside of Innsbruck.

By January, though, Arnold was back in the U.S. and alone. Brigitte eventually married his arch-rival Sylvester Stallone and starred in two of his films, *Rocky IV* and *Cobra*. On August 10, 1985, Arnold announced his en-

gagement to Maria Shriver. The wedding was set for April 26, 1986.

Probably aware his latest film was going to bomb at the box office, Arnold did no promotion for *Red Sonja*. Critics complained that despite Fleischer's professionalism, the movie had no style or tone, and that Nielsen couldn't act. "Bubbleheaded" and "shamelessly silly" were two of the epithets used to describe the plot, although it isn't much sillier than its Conan predecessors. "Even the horses wear too much junk jewelry," said Janet Maslin. The problem was that the core audience for S & S epics is young males, who are not particularly interested in the heroic exploits of the opposite sex.

In his next film, *Commando*, Arnold moved back into safer territory. The challenge was to find a way to make this movie stand out from the many others in the action/

Opposite: *Joel Silver produced* Commando *(1985), in which Arnold plays a retired Army colonel whose daughter (Alyssa Milano) is kidnapped by his enemies.*

Right: Arnold's co-star in Commando *is Rae Dawn Chong, daughter of comedian Tommy Chong of Cheech and Chong fame.*

Bottom right: Commando *combines humor with violence, epitomized by the weapons supermarket, Surplus World, where Arnold shops for his guns.*

adventure genre. Bruce Lee and Chuck Norris still had the martial arts market cornered, while Clint Eastwood, Charles Bronson and Sylvester Stallone reigned over the more general mayhem categories.

"I've always loved Clint Eastwood, Burt Reynolds and Charles Bronson because they were multimillion-dollar actors," Arnold said. "Eastwood and Reynolds are always battling to see who sells the most tickets, and I admire that, because the most important thing to me is to sell tickets."

Sylvester Stallone was another story. Stallone had captured the box office with *Rocky* and his 1982 Rambo movie *First Blood*, and was making a Rambo sequel. "Of course *Rambo* and *Commando* have a lot in common," said *Commando* producer Joel Silver. "They are both larger than life stories about cartoon-like characters that take on enormous odds and win."

"He [Stallone] just hits me the wrong way," Arnold told *Playboy*. "Whatever he does, it always comes out wrong. There's nothing that anyone can do out there to save his a– and his image." Some of the rivalry might have been because *Rambo: First Blood Part II* beat *Commando* into the movie theaters in 1985 and became one of the top hits of the summer.

The director for *Commando* was Mark L. Lester, a seasoned B-movie professional who was known for the power of action scenes in movies like *Stunts*. For romantic interest, the film uses Rae Dawn Chong, one of Hollywood's second-generation stars whose father Tommy Chong parlayed a running gag about two potheads into a successful career with Cheech Marin. After her 1982 debut in *Quest For Fire*, the epic about a prehistoric tribe, Chong was a hot property.

The rest of the cast, including Dan Hedaya (Arius), Vernon Wells (Bennett) and David Patrick Kelly (Sully),

Above: *Comic one-liners, a hallmark of* Commando*, soften the violence.*

Right: *By the time* Commando *was made, Arnold's $25 Cuban cigars had become a signature.*

Opposite: *Some critics complained about* Commando*, pointing out that a barracks blows up before Arnold has the time to plant explosives. But the fans loved it and made it one of the most popular movies of the year.*

had earned their chops in the action genre. Hedaya worked with Clint Eastwood in *Tightrope*, Wells with Mel Gibson in *The Road Warrior* and Kelly in *The Warriors* and *48 Hours*.

A script that was tailor-made for Arnold's talents helps account for *Commando*'s success at the box office. Arnold's Col. John Matrix has retired to the California hills with his daughter Jenny (Alyssa Milano). When Jenny is kidnapped by former confederate Bennett, Arnold goes on a one-man rampage.

The threatened-child formula makes a perfect rationale for mega-mayhem, and the boyish Chong is a good comic foil but not too seductive to get in the way of the action. One-liners fly fast and furiously.

The light tone is set very early when, after some very violent set-up scenes, Arnold appears chopping wood. He sees a reflection in the blade of his ax, spins and confronts not a villain, but his daughter. Arnold's favorite punchline comes in the final shoot-out. "Let off some steam," he tells Bennett, after impaling him with a steam pipe. One of the best sight gags in the movie has Arnold and Chong shopping for their weapons at a paramilitary supermarket called Surplus World.

Getting the right balance of humor and serious action was not easy. "The problem is that I can't go all out being funny because my daughter is in jeopardy," Arnold explained. "The trick is to say the funny lines without appearing to have fun. When I am asked about a man whom I've killed and I say, 'Don't disturb him, he's dead tired,' there has to be a serious look on my face."

Commando went into distribution in October 1985 and grossed $16.9 million in eleven days, but it didn't outdraw *Rambo: First Blood II*. Arnold went after Stallone in the press, insisting, "I'd be angry at hearing my name mentioned in the same breath as Stallone's. Stallone uses body doubles for some of the close-ups in his movies. I don't." He also criticized *Rambo II*. "We probably kill more people in *Commando* than Stallone did in *Rambo*, but the difference is that we don't pretend the violence is justified by patriotic pride. All that flag waving is a lot of bull. . . . I've made a better film than Stallone's, and I'm happy to wait for time to prove me right."

The critics had a few complaints of their own – about *Commando*. Although D.J.R. Bruckner of the *New York Times* thought the hero had sequel potential, he said, "Even a cinematic comic book needs more artful care than this was given." *Premiere* complained about the lack of fire in the romantic plot involving Rae Dawn Chong and reported that Arnold's one love scene with her had to be cut because Arnold was so tentative.

Still, Arnold won praise. "He has obviously been taking lessons as a stuntman, as well as in karate, fencing, knife-fighting and other manly arts, and he is more supple and faster in *Commando* than he ever has been," said Bruckner. "Swift, deliberate movement is a welcome addition to what in his other films was often only the most awesome physique in the world."

Arnold told *Time*, "Ten years ago, muscles were the most important thing. People knew me for one thing: bodybuilding. They wanted to see me with the muscles. But eventually I think they will forget about the 'Body'." Arnold had set a new goal for himself. He was smart enough not to stop making movies that built on the basis of his fame, but he was ready to experiment.

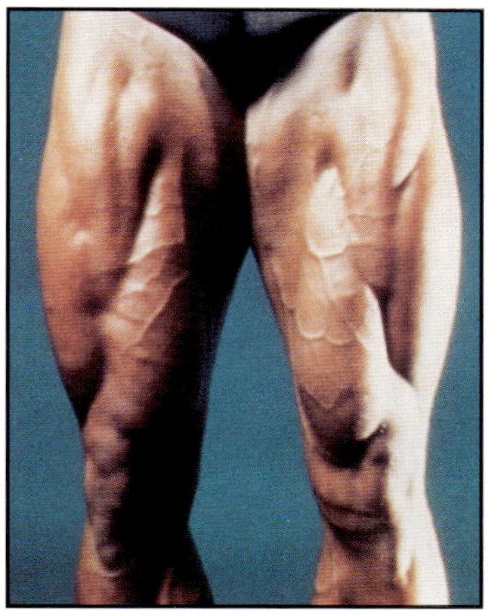

A QUARTET OF TOUGH-GUY MOVIES: *RAW DEAL* TO *RED HEAT* (1986-88)

Arnold has always known where he was heading next. After *Commando*'s release, he told the media, "The thing that separates me from the rest of the action leads, like Stallone, Eastwood and Norris, is that I bring in all this humor to my films. I love that, to have all this intensity, and then all of a sudden there is a funny line and you can relax." His next four films gave him a variety of ways to show off his talents as a tough guy with a sense of humor.

Before he was 30, Arnold had made a fortune. The accompanying financial security meant he could consider what movie projects to undertake without worrying about putting food on the table. "In the beginning, when people came to me and said, 'I have a great part for you where you play a truck driver and you're on screen for ten minutes, but we'll use your body,' I could afford to say no, because I didn't need the $20,000 they offered. It meant nothing to me," he said. "What I wanted to do was to build a career."

He kept his eyes firmly planted on the bottom line,

Opposite: *Reviewers compared* Raw Deal *to Arnold's arch rival Sylvester Stallone's* Cobra *– both released in 1986 – and called Arnold "the thinking kid's Sylvester Stallone."*

Right: *Arnold sported a new, slicked-back hair style and custom suits for* Raw Deal. *Critics called it a classier version of* Commando. *Appearing with him is Kathryn Harrold, who starred in the 1982 thriller* The Sender.

Left: Raw Deal *has its share of one-liners as well as guns. When Arnold's wife throws a cake at him, he tells her, "You should not drink and bake."*

Opposite: *Although Arnold had a fancy wardrobe for* Raw Deal*, he still stripped down for the action scenes. Cinematography was by Alex Thompson.*

though. "I'm a businessman," he said. "I'm interested in the movie making money. I'm not hung up on being an actor's actor or doing what they call artistic movies."

Raw Deal, another collaboration with De Laurentiis, continues the move towards humanizing the Austrian Oak but keeps Arnold squarely inside the action/adventure genre. "I feel I *like* to specialize in action/adventure films right now," he said. "I know that a lot of people say, 'I don't want to be typecast,' but that's crap. It's *all* typecasting. If they want a black guy for a movie, no matter how fantastic an actor you are, if you're white, you will not be hired. Not even if you're Dustin Hoffman. And if they want somebody ordinary-looking for *Kramer vs. Kramer*, they're not going to hire Sylvester Stallone and they're not going to hire me, because we don't look ordinary."

"I'm good if given the right role," he told *Rolling Stone*. "I know what I can do and can't. But I'm very happy with my work. I hope that each movie is on-the-job training and that they get better and better."

Raw Deal reflected a move away from movies that used only Arnold's physique. "Things are changing slowly," he told *The Saturday Evening Post*. "For instance my wardrobe in *Conan* cost four dollars, while for *Raw Deal* I got 20 expensive suits made in Beverly Hills. The bill for the baby oil for that film was very low, while on *Conan* it was very high. In fact, once during *Conan* when we shot in California, I had so much baby oil on that I slipped and fell into Nevada."

Filming for *Raw Deal* began in Chicago on November 1, 1985. It was a propitious time in Arnold's life. With his wedding to Maria Shriver less than six months away, he bought a $5 million, Spanish-style estate in Pacific Palisades, just north of Los Angeles. Lavishly appointed with seven bedrooms and four bathrooms, it also had a swimming pool, gym, tennis courts, two acres of gardens and a stream. His neighbors were actors John Forsythe and for a while, apparently, Sylvester Stallone and Brigitte Nielsen.

In *Raw Deal* Arnold plays Kaminsky, a cashiered FBI agent who agrees to help out his former boss Harry Shannon (Darren "Night Stalker" McGavin), after Shannon's son is murdered by the mob. Kaminsky fakes his death so he can leave behind his alcoholic wife Amy (Blanche Baker) and his job as a small town police chief to go undercover. He infiltrates the crime organization headed by Lou Patrovita (Sam Wanamaker), alternately cozying up to and outfoxing Patrovita's lieutenants – Rocca (Paul Shenar), and Max (Robert Davi). Kathryn Harrold plays Monique, the gangster's moll and undercover agent whom Arnold's Kaminsky toys with but never actually beds.

Although less campy than *Commando, Raw Deal* has a number of Arnold-style comic touches. In his first scene, he outwits an escaping motorcyclist by lighting a cigar and tossing it into a puddle of gasoline that explodes just as the cyclist rides into it. The best joke in the movie comes when Arnold and love-interest Harrold move to the bedroom after a lot of champagne. Harrold takes off Arnold's shirt. Then the camera cuts to Arnold's massive chest as Harrold exclaims, "Oh, my God," and Arnold passes out.

Arnold's scenes with Harrold caused a disagreement with De Laurentiis. The producer insisted the flirtation with Harrold's Monique should be consummated despite Kaminsky's marriage. Arnold thought otherwise. "That is you, Dino. Not me," Arnold said. "I want to be bigger in films that I am in life, not smaller."

Englishman John Irvin, whose expertise was not confined to macho action/adventure films, directed. Irvin had just finished the much-praised *Turtle Diary*, about two introverts (Glenda Jackson and Ben Kingsley) determined to free a set of sea turtles. The screenplay for *Raw Deal* was written by Gary M. DeVore, who did the script for Irvin's *Dogs of War*, and Norman Wexler, who wrote *Serpico*.

The supporting cast for *Raw Deal* was extensive. Kathryn Harrold had worked with Albert Brooks in *Modern Romance*, and with Jeff Goldblum and Michelle Pfeiffer in *Into the Night*. Ed Lauter, who plays the cop Baker, had appeared in films ranging from Hitchcock's *Family Plot* to three Bronson vehicles including *Death*

Wish III. Joe Regalbuto, who plays the crooked prosecutor, has been one of the regulars on TV's "Murphy Brown." Steven Hill, who plays the rival mobster Lamanski, appeared in *Rich and Famous, Yentl* and *Heartburn*. Paul Shenar was featured in Brian De Palma's *Scarface*, and Sam Wanamaker, who appeared in *Those Magnificent Men in Their Flying Machines* and *The Spy Who Came In From the Cold*, was also a director.

Raw Deal was released June 6, 1986. Although not quite the hit that *Commando* had been, it did well. Vincent Canby said, "The former Mr. Universe wears well as a film personality, partly because there's something comic about the massiveness of his frame and the genteelness of his manners [when in repose]." The *New York Daily News* said, "Schwarzenegger is a considerably appealing presence in pictures like this. May he make many more."

Premiere complained, however, that the attempt to provide him with a home life was a maudlin impediment to the action. David Denby said, "Speaking at a deliberate, Eastwoodish pace, he [Arnold] tried to be debonair in John Irvin's nifty, semi-satirical thriller ... and the attempt only half-worked."

In April, while shooting his next film, *Predator*, Arnold had flown directly from Puerto Vallarta, Mexico, to the Kennedy compound at Hyannis Port, Massachusetts, for his spectacular wedding to Maria Shriver. In attendance were Senator Ted Kennedy, Jacqueline Kennedy Onassis and other members of the Kennedy clan, as well as Oprah Winfrey, Andy Warhol and Grace Jones.

Left and below: *Arnold married Maria Shriver in Hyannis Port, MA on April 26, 1986.*

Opposite: *In* Predator *(1986), Arnold plays a former C.I.A. operative sent to Central America.*

Arnold's wedding gift to Maria was a silk-screened portrait of her by Warhol.

Predator's plot features Arnold as Dutch, who teams up with a former C.I.A. buddy Dillon (Carl Weathers) to lead mercenaries into a Central American nation. That mission accomplished, Arnold finds himself slogging through the jungle with a mysterious monster in pursuit. The monster, who has a penchant for skinning men alive, is played by Kevin Peter Hall, fresh from his role as Big Foot in *Harry and the Hendersons*, and seems to be a mix of Indian totem and extraterrestrial. He is able to disappear into the jungle background with the flip of a special effects switch, and when wounded, leaves behind iridescent green blood.

One by one, the predator picks off the members of the combat team, including Hawkins (Shane Black), Billy (Sonny Landham), Blain (Jesse Ventura) and Poncho (Richard Chaves). Eventually only Dutch (Arnold) and Anna (Elpidia Carrillo), a native they've captured along the way, are left. Arnold does battle with the mean green monster and outwits him singlehandedly.

The Arnold signatures are in place by the first scene: $25 Cuban Davidoff stogie (from *Raw Deal*) and sunglasses (from *The Terminator*). There are plenty of one-liners as well. "Stick around," Arnold tells an opponent after impaling him with a knife. Then, just before kicking in a door, "Knock, knock."

Director John McTiernan had at the time a single undistinguished film credit in addition to *Predator*. He went on, however, to make two hits, *Die Hard* with Bruce Willis and *The Hunt for Red October* with Sean Connery.

Predator's supporting cast included R.G. Armstrong, veteran of *The Fugitive Kind, El Dorado* and *Ride the High Country*, playing the general who launches the mission. Sonny Landham had appeared in *48 Hours* as well as other less popular shoot-em-ups, and Elpidia

Above: *Kevin Peter Hall plays the Predator.*

Below: *Dillon is played by Carl Weathers.*

Opposite: The Running Man*'s emcee Richard Dawson hosted TV's popular game show "Family Feud" in real life.*

Carrillo had made a career out of playing victimized Hispanic women in movies like *The Border* and *Salvador*.

Despite its confused and meandering plot, *Predator* racked up another success at the box office. Director McTiernan had praise for his star. "The range of things he can do is expanding daily," McTiernan said. "I had been warned that I'd have to do 112 takes for him to act it right, but that's just not so. We've never gone more than nine, and four of those were for camera problems and two because Arnold and another actor would break out laughing. The guy could be another John Wayne."

Critic Janet Maslin found the movie alternately grisly and dull, but fans didn't. *Predator* grossed $34.9 million within the first three weeks of its release, and the National Association of Theater Owners named Arnold 1987 Star of the Year.

For his next feature, Arnold returned to science fiction. He began filming *The Running Man* in the first part of 1987. Steven E. de Souza, who wrote the script for *48 Hours*, adapted Stephen King's novel for the screen (Richard Bachman is King's nom de plume). It recalls both the 1975 movie *Rollerball* and the short story "The Most Dangerous Game" by Richard Connell.

In 2019, the United States has been taken over by a fascist government that controls the populace with television. "The Running Man" is a popular TV game show that helps keep the public off the streets. Arnold plays Ben Richards, a federal policeman who disobeys orders to end a food riot by killing everyone in sight. As a result of this humane gesture, he is falsely accused of being the "Butcher of Bakersfield" and ends up as sport for the mob on "The Running Man." Emcee Damon Killian is gleefully played by Richard Dawson, host of one of TV's real-life game shows, "Family Feud."

Arnold fends off a variety of awesomely futuristic gladiators. Fireball (former Cleveland Browns fullback Jim Brown) wields a flamethrower. Captain Freedom (Jesse Ventura, fresh from his role as Blain in *Predator*) becomes the butt of one of the movie's best jokes when Killian says to him, "What's the matter, steroids make you deaf?" Dynamo (Erland Van Lidth) is an operatic brute who lights up like a Christmas tree, Buzzsaw (Gus Rethwisch) wields a chainsaw, and Subzero (Toru Tanaka) is a hockey player with a razor-edged stick.

Arnold bests them all with a lot of muscle and a few bonmots. "Follow me, lightbulb," he taunts Dynamo. Later, when he immolates Fireball with his own gas tank, Arnold quips, "What a hothead."

Director Paul Michael Glaser was no stranger to action/adventure. He played Starsky in the TV cop show "Starsky and Hutch," and his first feature as a director, *Band of the Hand* (1986), was about five convicts trained to be cops.

Headlining the supporting cast after Jim Brown was character actor Yaphet Kotto (Laughlin). Kotto had appeared in everything from the 1973 James Bond epic

Above: *A successful sci-fi satire of television, 1987's* The Running Man *offered Arnold's characteristic combination of action, humor, and violence.*

Left: *One of Arnold's many adversaries in* The Running Man *is chainsaw-wielding Buzzsaw, played by Gus Rethwisch.*

Opposite top: *In* Red Heat *(1988), Arnold plays a Soviet cop bent on capturing a Soviet drug dealer.*

Opposite bottom: *Arnold smokes his trademark Davidoff in front of the Kremlin.* Red Heat *was the first American film in which location work was done in Moscow's Red Square.*

Live and Let Die to *Alien* and *Midnight Run*. Although less of an afterthought than Elpidia Carrillo in *Predator*, Maria Conchita Alonso (Amber Mendes) comes along as extra baggage caught up in the general mayhem. Her first movie credit, *Moscow on the Hudson*, gave her high visibility, and she later worked with Robert Duval and Sean Penn in *Colors*. Musician Frank Zappa's son Dweezil put in an appearance as Stevie.

The Running Man was released in November 1987, and became one of the winter's biggest moneymakers. Audience surveys showed the largest percentage of female interest in Arnold yet. When Arnold asked why, he learned that women wrote down they liked his derrière. "That's really helpful," Arnold joked. "Now I know which direction to take with my next movie."

As usual, the critics were less than enthusiastic. Vincent Canby said it "has the manners and the gadgetry of a sci-fi adventure film but is, at heart, an engagingly mean, cruel, nasty, funny send-up of television."

Arnold argued that *The Running Man* had less violence than many of his films. "The cameras focus more on the faces and show the fear and the tension," he said. "Still, people get entertained in different ways. Some like love stories, some like historical movies, some like emotional films. And then there is that category of people who just like to go and see action movies with some violence throughout."

Winning an Academy Award has never been a top priority for Arnold. "The Oscar is only one way of establishing yourself," he said. "You can establish yourself as the actor who makes the most money for the studio. Or the one who actually receives the highest salary. Or the one who has the biggest percentage of ownership of the film. Like Clint Eastwood, for instance. He has a unique deal. He is truly the king of the film industry and the box office world-wide." If he wasn't winning awards for his acting, Arnold was getting other forms of recognition. On June 2, 1987, star #1847 was placed on Hollywood Boulevard with Arnold's name on it.

Arnold began work on a new film, *Red Heat*, in 1988. This time he plays Soviet cop Ivan Danko, who teams up with wise-mouthed, laissez-faire Chicago detective Art Ridzik (Jim Belushi) to pursue Soviet drug dealer Viktor (Ed O'Ross). At the director's request, Arnold lost ten to fifteen pounds for the film and worked with an accent coach to fine tune his Russian.

Co-star Belushi, who had starred in *Trading Places* and *Salvador*, was impressed with his partner. "He's a very intelligent actor," Belushi said. "I called him the Professor. Off screen, he did all the talking. He taught me about finance, real estate, publicity."

Red Heat starts in Russia with a scene in a health club, complete with weightlifters and steam baths, where Arnold confronts the Russian drug dealer. Arnold appears stark naked except for a small towel worn like an apron. The fight that starts in the steam room ends up outside in five feet of snow. The scene was filmed in Schladming, an Austrian town outside Graz, where Arnold had grown up. When one of Arnold's stuntmen, Bennie Dobbins, died of a heart attack, Arnold cancelled plans to attend the annual Vienna Opera Ball with his mother and Maria. The film is dedicated to Dobbins. Later, *Red Heat* made history when the cast filmed in

Moscow's Red Square. It was the first time an American movie company had been allowed to shoot there.

Director Walter Hill, an accomplished B-movie director, had turned out a variety of powerful action/adventure films, including *The Warriors, The Long Riders* and *48 Hours.* He liked working with Arnold. "He's more than an actor. He's a natural force," the director said. "Arnold's secret is his face. It's the face of a medieval warrior – a face with great natural dignity and an almost regal quality." Hill's tactic in the film is to let Belushi do the talking. Arnold reacts with his face.

Once Belushi and Arnold team up, the movie tries to build a contrast between Belushi's lackadaisical style and Arnold's no-nonsense, authoritarian approach to police work. Peter Boyle, an actor probably best known as the monster in *Young Frankenstein*, plays Belushi's boss Lou Connelly. Gina Gershon provides the female interest as Viktor's mail-order American bride.

The emphasis is on fists, guns and other forms of violence. "When you make an Arnold movie," Hill said, "you're not exactly thinking about the refined sensibilities of the *New York Times.*" Arnold defended the film as more than a shallow shoot-em-up. "The guy I play learns from America," he said. "And though he makes friends here, he goes proudly back to his own land. It's not one more script in which a Russian defects."

When *Red Heat* opened on June 17, 1988, the box office returns were disappointing, especially considering that Arnold had reportedly been paid $10 million. The *Village Voice* called the movie a rip-off of *48 Hours* and said it "achieves new dimensions in soulless machismo." *Films and Filming* suggested "the big mistake was making *Red Heat* such a relentlessly straight crime drama." *Red Heat* needed more comedy, and Arnold's next film delivered.

Above: *Early in* Red Heat, *Arnold is confronted in a steam bath.*

Opposite top left: *Arnold worked with a coach on his Russian accent.*

Opposite top right: *Co-star Jim Belushi is the late comedian John Belushi's brother.*

Opposite bottom: *Arnold called his character a male version of Ninotchka.*

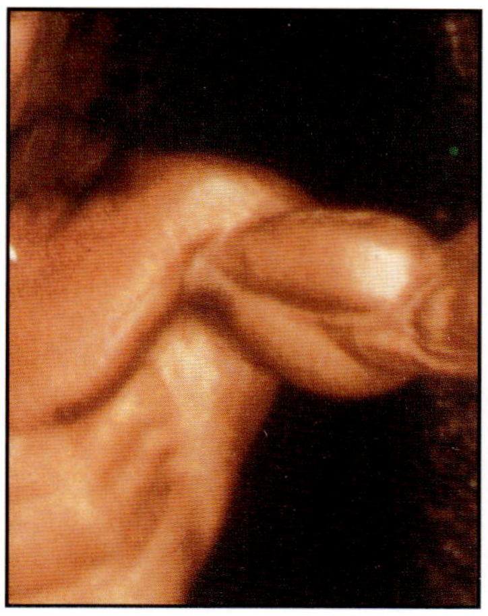

EXPANDING HORIZONS, SMASHING SUCCESS: *TWINS* TO *TERMINATOR 2* (1988-91)

Arnold's move into comedy resulted in his biggest box office hit ever: *Twins*. The new Arnold was kinder and gentler. "People will finally understand why you married Arnold," *Twins* director Ivan Reitman said to Maria Shriver at the movie's premiere.

Planning for *Twins* began in 1985 when, after meeting Ivan Reitman, Arnold took the director aside and said he wanted to do a movie with him. Reitman's string of comedies – *Meatballs, Stripes, Ghostbusters, Ghostbusters II*, featuring former "Saturday Night Live" star Bill Murray, had made him one of Hollywood's more bankable comedy directors. Reitman commissioned a group of screenwriters to come up with concepts appropriate for Arnold. The best of the bunch was the *Twins* script, written by William Davies, William Osborne, Timothy Harris and Herschel Weingrod.

In *Twins*, a genetics lab hatches the perfect human specimen, named Julius Benedict (Arnold), by insem-

Opposite: *The unlikely teaming of Arnold with diminutive actor/director Danny DeVito resulted in the hit comedy* Twins.

Right: *The script for* Twins *was hand tailored to suit Arnold by director Ivan Reitman, known for Bill Murray vehicles such as the smash hit* Ghostbusters.

Overleaf: Twins *co-star Kelly Preston, who plays Marnie, also appears in "The Switch," which Arnold directed for HBO.*

Opposite: *Arnold tried his first song and dance in* Twins.

Above: *Arnold on the campaign trail with George Bush in 1988 in Chicago.*

inating a superwoman with the sperm of six ideal men. The only catch is that the experiment also produces a twin brother, Vincent (Danny DeVito), who is Julius's opposite. On their 35th birthday, Julius sets out to find his nefarious lost brother. The two join forces to stumble through a series of misadventures involving sisters – one for each of the brothers – Linda (Chloe Webb) and Marnie (Kelly Preston), a stolen jet fuel injection system, and the search for Julius's and Vincent's mother.

When Arnold and Reitman met to discuss the concept, Reitman was only halfway through explaining it before Arnold said, "When do we start?" To get the project going, both the director and the two stars suspended their usual fees for a large cut of the gross. "One thing I realized," Arnold said, "was that I really enjoyed doing comedy, but there would always be confrontations with the directors, with the studios. 'Naw, naw, naw. What we want you to do is to be a tough guy.' I was trying to figure out how I could do a comedy from beginning to end."

Shooting for *Twins* began in California in spring 1988, with trips to New Mexico for location work. Arnold's costar Danny DeVito has credits ranging from *One Flew Over the Cuckoo's Nest* to *Ruthless People*. DeVito has also worked as a director, with such hits as *Throw Momma From the Train* and *The War of the Roses*. DeVito's romantic partner for the movie, Chloe Webb, was a veteran of the TV series "China Beach" and won praise for her performance in *Sid and Nancy*.

Arnold's movie girlfriend Kelly Preston had appeared in a variety of low-budget comedies and teen movies. Professional Southerner Trey Wilson (*Raising Arizona, Bull Durham*) is the nasty corporate thief Beetroot McKinley, while assorted scientists and bad guys are played by Marshall Bell, Hugh O'Brian, Nehemiah Persoff, Maury Chaykin, Thom McCleister and David Efron. Maria Shriver had a walk-on part as a woman who buys flowers, although the scene didn't make the final edit.

When the studio tested the movie, Arnold reported that "the real hard-core Arnold audience felt that this was the best movie I've even done. It shows frustrations. It shows up and downs. A lot of caring." He had a theory, "that all the things the audience does not expect from a big guy work ten times better when you do them because they don't expect it."

Some scenes needed to be choreographed, however. When the camera cut to a reaction shot after Julius had lost his virginity, Reitman instructed Arnold simply to stare at a fixed point from flat on the ground. The director then arranged Arnold's expression muscle by muscle. "He has extraordinary physical control," Reitman said, "and it extends to his face."

One of the more difficult scenes for Arnold involved a gag on a plane in which he sings the 1950s hit "Yakety Yak" while plugged into a Walkman. Not a singer, Arnold produced nevertheless. "The key there," Reitman explained, "was to let him be absolutely open – to strip all the acting away and let himself come through." Clint Eastwood came to the set for Arnold's singing debut and with tongue in cheek told him, "I didn't know you had so much talent."

Arnold's erstwhile rival Sylvester Stallone gets a nod

Left: *With a clever plot premise,* Total Recall *turned into a 1990 summer blockbuster.*

Opposite left: *Arnold plays a construction worker whose haunting dreams about life on Mars turn out to be true.*

Opposite right: *Much of* Total Recall *is set in Venusville, a ghetto for horrific mutants such as a three-breasted prostitute.*

Overleaf: *In order to escape to Mars, Arnold disguises himself as a woman. When he is discovered, a fight ensues and leads to collapse of the pressurized atmosphere in the airport.*

in the film. Passing a giant poster of Stallone as Rambo, Julius does a doubletake and shakes his head. Listed in the credits are thanks to Stallone. Singer Nicolette Larson makes a brief appearance, singing in a bar. Other music in the movie is performed by Little Richard, 2 Live Crew with the Coasters, and Bobby McFarrin and Herbie Hancock.

Twins premiered at the Kennedy Center in Washington, D.C., on December 5, 1988, and led the box office for its first two weekends, grossing $22.2 million in ten days and ultimately over $110 million. Proceeds from the movie's premiere went to the Special Olympics. One of the more illustrious guests at the premiere was President-Elect George Bush. Despite his marriage to a member of the Kennedy clan, Arnold has been an ardent Republican since he became a U.S. citizen in 1983. A Nixon and Reagan supporter, he attended the Republican National Convention in both 1984 and 1988 and campaigned for Bush in the fall of 1988.

Bush took advantage of his speech for the *Twins* premiere to josh Arnold. "There are all kinds of courage," the President-Elect said. "There is the courage of

my friend Arnold Schwarzenegger, who more than once campaigned with me across this country – and then returned home each time to take the heat from his own in-laws."

As Arnold raked in the money, some critics expressed dismay. Janet Maslin called *Twins* "sad evidence that witty direction is becoming a dying art." Martin Sutton of *Films and Filming* said, "Arnie's grimly one-note acting style is like a lead weight around the production." Jami Bernard in *Video* magazine warned, "Schwarzenegger may get laughs in his action flicks from his martini-dry one-liners, but he is not ready to be paired with DeVito, whose height belies his strength, which is enough to carry a film."

Richard Schickel was more positive. Writing in *Time*, he said "Both stars are expert at playing dumb in highly contrasting ways and their search for their mother has its touching aspects." Jim Kozak of *Boxoffice* called it the best performance of Arnold's career, saying, "Arnold's trademark teutonic scowl has been replaced at last by a conspicuously sunny disposition, and his warmth and guileless delivery are completely on-target throughout."

Arnold had guessed right again. "I think *Twins* is going to have a surprising impact," he said in an interview just after the movie's release. "It's going to be good for my career because I can then do more of the movies I would like to do. Which is to do more comedies like that and then do movies like *California Suite* [the Neil Simon comedy]."

His next feature, however, was not a comedy. *Total Recall* is a sci-fi movie of the New Bad Future variety. Mixing character elements of ordinary nice guy and superhero, it seemed tailor-made for Arnold. Even more so than with *Twins*, Arnold had control over the design of the package. He struck a deal with Carolco Pictures that gave him approval of script, director, costars and the marketing campaign.

For the time *Total Recall* was, at close to $60 million, one of the most expensive films ever made. Only *Rambo III* cost more. Upstart Carolco Pictures had a reputation for both big spending and foreign market development, a combination that clearly appealed to Arnold. "I don't want to make a decision to work hard at something, to believe in something one hundred percent and then have an executive in there who doesn't believe in spending a lot of money," he said.

The script for *Total Recall* had been floating around Hollywood for almost ten years. Based on a story by science fiction writer Philip K. Dick called "We Can Remember It for You Wholesale," the plot involves an ordinary working man whose memory of his identity as a Mars-based secret agent has been erased. Writers Ronald Shusett and Dan O'Bannon, who had done the

Above: *Sharon Stone plays Arnold's phony wife Lori, who is really a Cohaagen operative.*

Opposite: *Rachel Ticotin plays Melina, Arnold's girlfriend on Mars.*

script for *Alien*, made a deal with Disney in 1979 to write *Total Recall*, but it foundered. Arnold learned about the project after Dino De Laurentiis bought it in 1982, but it languished when the producer was unwilling to pay Arnold enough or to give him director approval.

Between 1982 and 1989, the script went through 50 drafts, five directors (including Fred Schepisi and David Cronenberg), three more studios and two other leading men (Richard Dreyfuss and Patrick Swayze). When De Laurentiis's company went out of business, Arnold persuaded Carolco to snap up the script at a bargain price. An admirer of Paul Verhoeven's violent thriller *Robocop*, Arnold invited the Dutch filmmaker to direct the movie.

Filming for *Total Recall* took place in Mexico at the Churubusco Studios. Vic Armstrong, who had worked as Harrison Ford's double in the Indiana Jones movies, was in charge of stunts, and makeup artist Jefferson Dawn created much of the gore as well as the disfigured mutants who play a crucial role in the story.

As Doug Quaid, Arnold has not one, but two love interests. The villain Cohaagen (Ronny Cox) who erased his memory has provided him with a phony wife Lori (Sharon Stone), and he has a girlfriend on Mars, Melina (Rachel Ticotin). Quaid pays a visit to the futuristic travel agency Rekall, Inc, where Dr. Lull (Rosemary Dunsmore) implants memories of a vacation to Mars and accidentally discovers he has another identity. With bad guy Richter (Michael Ironside) in pursuit, he heads to Mars, where he finds and aids an underground resistance group headed by Kuato (Marshall Bell, who played Webster in *Twins*).

Former dancer Rachel Ticotin had appeared in *Fort Apache, the Bronx* with Paul Newman. Beginning with *Deadly Blessing*, Sharon Stone appeared in a variety of action-oriented films, including the remake of *King Solomon's Mines* with Richard Chamberlain. Ronny Cox worked with Verhoeven in *Robocop*, and Michael Ironside, the evil Richter, was featured in *Top Gun*.

Despite the greater attention paid to romance, Arnold hardly topples Valentino in *Total Recall*. The script does provide a vehicle that is subtler and more complex than his previous films, and he reaches a new level of confi-

Left: *The memory machine into which Arnold is strapped is reminiscent of Dr. Frankenstein's laboratory devices.*

Opposite top: *Kuato, the elusive leader of the Martian underground, is played by Marshall Bell.*

Opposite bottom: *Arnold and Melina rescue the Martian population at the conclusion of* Total Recall.

dence as an actor. "A dialogue scene used to make me nervous," he said. "I can see it in my face in my old movies. I feel much more comfortable with gentle scenes than violent ones. . . . In real life, I was always working more on being gentle and courteous, because of the body."

Although *Total Recall* dishes out the usual diet of Arnold violence and revenge, it also makes tantalizing attempts at social commentary. Arnold's Quaid is a man of the people, whose sympathies move instinctively to the Martian mutants who comprise the underclass of the future. The movie's plot has to do with control of natural resources, a highly relevant issue for the environmentally-concerned 1990s. Like most sci-fi movies *Total Recall* has misogynist undercurrents, but Arnold's two co-stars, Rachel Ticotin and Sharon Stone, are hardly shrinking violets. The movie seems to try to appeal on two levels, wallowing in crudity and gore at the same time as it raises serious moral and political questions.

Above left: *A certain sign of Arnold's arrival at the pinnacle of movie success was the installation of his star on Hollywood Boulevard in 1987.*

Above: *As Chairman of the President's Council on Physical Fitness and Sports, Arnold appeared at a sports fitness demonstration with President George Bush on the grounds of the White House in 1990.*

Left: *Arnold's first daughter, Katherine Eunice, was born in December 1989.*

Opposite: *Some of the elements in Arnold's life were reflected in his role as a policeman who goes undercover as a kindergarten teacher in* Kindergarten Cop *(1990).*

At the center of the movie is a fairly standard vision of a nightmare future dehumanized by technology, overpopulation and possible nuclear destruction. In the 2084 A.D. world of *Total Recall*, Quaid neutralizes the nightmare by siding with the disadvantaged in Venusville and starting up the nuclear reactor that will provide them with air.

During the movie, Quaid struggles to recover his memory and discover through it his true identity. "A man is defined by his actions, not his memory," Kuato, the telepathic resistance leader tells him. In the broader context of the movie, the statement is paradoxical. *Total Recall* ends with lines reminiscent of Hitchcock. Quaid says to Melina, "I just had a terrible thought. What if this is a dream?" Melina's answer to Quaid in the final scene, "Kiss me quick before you wake up," is the stuff of the Hollywood Dream Factory.

By the time it was released in the spring of 1990, Arnold had been named chairman of the President's Council on Physical Fitness and Sports by President Bush. With the birth of Katherine Eunice Schwarzenegger on December 13, 1989, he had also become a father. Commercial down to its sprocket holes, *Total Recall* features 28 different brand names shown a total of 55 times, drawing fire from Ralph Nader and the Center for the Study of Commercialism. *Total Recall* was one of the summer's big successes, with revenues of $91.4 million in the first month.

Critics were more impressed with Arnold than they had been in the past. *Boxoffice* said, "Genuinely original and achingly familiar at the same time, it should emerge as one of 1990's biggest hits." In the *Monthly Film Bulletin* of the British Film Institute, Kim Newman said, "Ingenious and entertaining rather than inspiring, *Total Recall* stands as state-of-the-art science fiction." Janet Maslin called it "a thunderous tribute to its star's determination to create, out of the unlikeliest raw materials, a patently synthetic yet surprisingly affable leading man." *Total Recall*'s special effects won an Oscar.

Arnold's next choice of movie seemed to mirror some of the changes going on in his personal life. In *Kindergarten Cop* he plays a policeman who goes undercover by becoming a kindergarten teacher. "For ten years, I have been telling writers, producers, directors, and studio executives that I would love to do a film where a kid or children are a very important part," he said. "Something like Jon Voight did in his boxing movie [*The Champ*]. You change always when you're around children."

Convincing Ivan Reitman to direct was not easy. When Universal Pictures sent the script to Arnold, he told them he would do it if Reitman, who had directed *Twins*, would. Reitman turned the project down. After a hard sell by Arnold and some negotiations over his participation in developing the script further, Reitman relented. As a result, secondary themes important to

Opposite: *Although it features a "kinder, gentler" Arnold,* Kindergarten Cop *contains heavy doses of violence.*

Right: *Penelope Ann Miller plays Arnold's romantic interest in* Kindergarten Cop.

Reitman were added concerning child abuse, broken homes, family life and romance.

The supporting cast for *Kindergarten Cop* was a classy line-up. Penelope Ann Miller (Joyce) worked with Marlon Brando in *The Freshman*. Pamela Reed (Arnold's partner Phoebe) appeared in *The Right Stuff* and *The Cadillac Man*, and starred in the TV sitcom "Grand." Linda Hunt (Miss Schlowski) starred in *The Year of Living Dangerously* with Mel Gibson. Richard Tyson (Crisp) appeared in the campy *Two Moon Junction*. Carroll Baker, as Crisp's nasty mother, won fame in such 1950s classics as *Baby Doll* and *Giant*.

Arnold celebrated his 43rd birthday on the set of *Kindergarten Cop* with 30 of the tots in the movie, as well as Maria, seven-month-old Katherine Eunice, and such personal friends as 1950s TV comedian Milton Berle. Arnold was surprised to discover how many of the children in the movie were familiar with earlier films such as *Predator, The Terminator* and *Twins*. Their appraisals of him were not necessarily worshipful, though. One little girl said, "Arnold is strange as a teacher. But I like him." "He picks his nose," said a five-year-old boy.

Kindergarten Cop did well at the box office, grossing $11.3 million in its first five days and more than $120 million overall, but critics complained about harsh language and violence. *Boxoffice* said, "Clearly this movie is intended for the whole family, but an apparent tussle between creating a new, huggable Arnold and maintaining his musclebound, crime-busting image has resulted in a film that is surprisingly rough in spots."

Arnold's next project made it clear that action and violence were not going to be banished from his movies. Rumors abounded about *Terminator 2: Judgment Day*'s gigantic budget of close to $100 million, reputed to be the most ever spent. Arnold told Arsenio Hall that the catering costs for *Terminator 2* were more than the entire $6.9 million price tag for the first *Terminator*. Arnold's paycheck was reputed to be a $14 million Gulfstream jet.

"The first *Terminator* was a very, very big stepping stone for me," Arnold said. "It helped me get out of that genre of muscle films like *Conan* and into legitimate action films. I've been offered a lot of money to do sequels to my other films, like *Predator* and *Commando*, but the only one I really wanted to do was *Terminator*."

Arnold was also adamant about working with director James Cameron again. Cameron had followed up *The Terminator* with the highly successful *Aliens* (1986). "He was demanding in 1984," Arnold said; "he's very demanding now." Cameron co-wrote the script for *Terminator 2* with William Wisher, and Adam Greenberg, who shot *The Terminator*, was director of photography.

"No one else could play the Terminator," Cameron said. "Arnold's really matured into the role." Arnold said, "Let's face it, he's the ultimate fantasy character. When he comes to a wall, he walks right through it.

Left: *In* Terminator 2: Judgment Day *(1991), Arnold returns as the Terminator, now assigned to protect young John Connor (Edward Furlong) against a new, deadly Terminator.*

Opposite: *During a summer when Hollywood suffered from anemic box office returns,* Terminator 2, *with a budget of close to $100 million, turned into a blockbuster.*

Everyone wishes he could do that." Much of the walking-through-walls is done by stuntmen, led by Gary Davis. Almost every scene in *Terminator 2: Judgment Day* involves a motorcycle, helicopter, fight or jump necessitating at least one stuntman. A total of 800 stuntman-days were used in the film, more than two and a half times the number used in *Indiana Jones and the Temple of Doom*.

Another unique characteristic of *Terminator 2* is the use of digital processing, a new special effects technology that allows the filmmakers to superimpose one image onto another and erase such devices as the wires or harnesses that make some stunts possible. Thanks to digital processing, one dangerous scene in which Arnold's Harley Davidson apparently leaps over a wall was shot with a double simply sitting on the motorcycle while it was slowly pulled over the wall on cables, later erased.

Arnold has a new role in the sequel. His Terminator becomes a good guy, swearing not to kill and helping to rescue a now half-grown John Connor (14-year-old Edward Furlong). A new evil Terminator (Robert Patrick), sent from the future to eliminate Connor, becomes the threat. "Because he's made out of liquid metal, he can literally go through anything," Arnold explained. "In other words, he really *is* indestructible and a much more threatening machine than I am. So I become, in a way, the outdated machine in this film."

Linda Hamilton, who as Sarah Connor ended *The Terminator* pregnant with the child who was destined to save the world, trained for three months for her part. "I strengthened and completely reshaped my body. If I

Opposite top: *Director James Cameron (second from left) and co-star Linda Hamilton (left) both returned to work on* Terminator 2.

Opposite bottom: *At the conclusion of* Terminator 2, *Arnold sends the new Terminator to a fiery end as John Connor and his mother Sarah look on.*

Right: *Robert Patrick plays the new Terminator, which is made of liquid metal and is capable of transforming into almost any shape.*

hadn't, who knows if I'd be alive today? The physical demands were incredible," Hamilton said. In *Terminator 2* Sarah has become a fanatical warrior after being incarcerated in a mental hospital because of her obsession with the Terminator.

Robert Patrick, who plays the new T-1000 model Terminator, is a Roger Corman alumnus. Joe Morton, as the scientist whose research could destroy the world, dies to save the human race. A veteran of stage and screen, Morton starred in *The Brother From Another Planet*.

Terminator 2: Judgment Day opened on July 3, 1991. Critics liked what they saw. "Mr. Cameron has made a swift, exciting special-effects epic that thoroughly justifies its vast expense and greatly improves upon the first film's potent but rudimentary visual style," said Janet Maslin. "Mr. Muscle delivers the explosive goods," said *U.S.A. Today*. Complaints focused on the murky plot and a peace theme contradicting the movie's violence.

If there had been any question before, *Terminator 2* put Arnold on top of the Hollywood heap. By the first week, box office returns were $52.3 million. Arnold already had his eyes fixed on a new challenge: directing. In an interview for *Terminator 2*, Arnold said, "Right now, my idol is Danny DeVito. That little guy stars in and directs his own movies. That's big in my book."

A year earlier, Arnold had gotten his first taste of being behind the camera, selecting an episode for the HBO horror anthology "Tales from the Crypt." The plot for "The Switch" involves a rich old man who falls in love with a beautiful young woman played by Kelly Preston (Marnie in *Twins*). The old man spends his fortune acquiring the perfect face and body, only to lose the girl in the end. It sounded like a nightmare Arnold could have dreamed up from his own life. The difference is that when it comes to the real world, Arnold has always known how to create happy endings for himself.

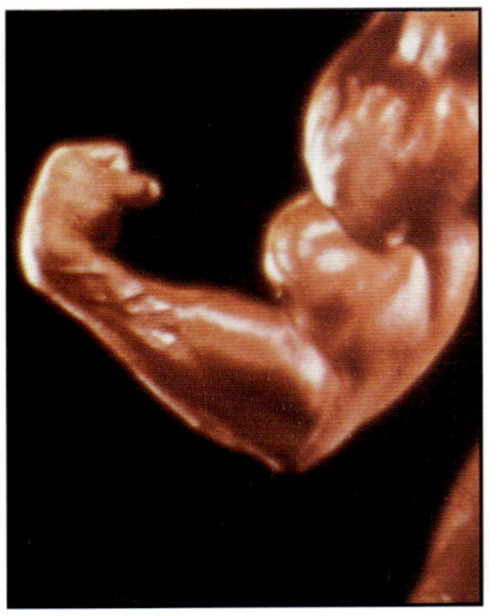

FILMOGRAPHY

1970 **Hercules in New York** (also released as *Hercules Goes Bananas* and *Hercules – the Movie*) RAF Industries, Arthur A. Seidelman (D) Arnold Strong (Schwarzenegger), Arnold Stang, Deborah Loomis.

1973 **The Long Goodbye** United Artists, Robert Altman (D) Elliott Gould, Sterling Hayden, Nina Van Pallandt, Henry Gibson, Mark Rydell, Jim Bouton, David Arkin, Warren Berlinger, David Carradine.

1976 **Stay Hungry** United Artists, Bob Rafelson (D) Jeff Bridges, Sally Field, R.G. Armstrong, Helena Kallianiotes, Roger E. Mosley.

1977 **Pumping Iron** (Documentary) Cinema 5, George Butler/Robert Fiore (D) Lou Ferrigno, Mike Katz, Mattie and Victoria Ferrigno.

1979 **The Villain** Columbia Pictures, Hal Needham (D) Kirk Douglas, Strother Martin, Paul Lynde, Ruth Buzzi, Jack Elam, Foster Brooks.

1980 **The Jayne Mansfield Story** (TV Movie) Dick Lowry (D) Loni Anderson, Raymond Buktenica, Kathleen Lloyd, G.D. Spradlin, Dave Shelley.

1980 **Mr. Olympia Bodybuilding Championships** (Video) American Sports Network, Frank Zane.

1982 **Conan the Barbarian** Universal, John Milius (D) Max Von Sydow, James Earl Jones, Sandahl Bergman, Mako.

1984 **Conan the Destroyer** Universal, Richard Fleischer (D) Grace Jones, Wilt Chamberlain, Sarah Douglas, Mako, Tracey Walter, Olivia d'Abo.

1984 **The Terminator** Orion Pictures, James Cameron (D) Paul Winfield, Michael Biehn, Linda Hamilton.

1985 **The Making of "The Terminator" and "Missing in Action 2"** (Video) Cannon, Chuck Norris, Michael Biehn, Linda Hamilton.

1985 **Red Sonja** MGM/UA Entertainment, Richard Fleischer (D) Brigitte Nielsen, Sandahl Bergman, Paul Smith, Ernie Reyes Jr., Ronald Lacey, Pat Roach.

1985 **Commando** Twentieth Century Fox, Mark L. Lester (D) Rae Dawn Chong, Dan Hedaya, Vernon Wells, David Patrick Kelly, Alyssa Milano, James Olson, Bill Duke.

1986 **Raw Deal** De Laurentiis Entertainment Group, John Irvin (D) Kathryn Harrold, Darren McGavin, Sam Wanamaker, Paul Shenar, Steven Hill, Joe Regalbuto, Robert Davi, Ed Lauter.

1987 **Predator** Twentieth Century Fox, John McTiernan (D) Jesse Ventura, Sonny Landham, Bill Duke, Elpidia Carrillo.

1987 **The Running Man** Tri-Star Pictures, Paul Michael Glaser (D) Richard Dawson, Maria Conchita Alonso, Yaphet Kotto, Mick Fleetwood, Dweezil Zappa, Jesse Ventura.

1988 **Red Heat** Tri-Star Pictures, Walter Hill (D) Jim Belushi, Peter Boyle, Ed O'Ross

1988 **Twins** Universal, Ivan Reitman (D) Danny DeVito, Kelly Preston, Bonnie Bartlett, Chloe Webb.

1990 **Total Recall** Tri-Star Pictures, Paul Verhoeven (D) Rachel Ticotin, Sharon Stone, Ronny Cox, Michael Ironside, Marshall Bell, Mel Johnson Jr., Roy Bjocksmith.

1990 **Kindergarten Cop** Universal, Ivan Reitman (D) Penelope Ann Miller, Pamela Reed, Linda Hunt, Richard Tyson, Carroll Baker, Joseph Cousins, Christian Cousins.

1991 **Terminator 2: Judgment Day** Tri-Star Pictures, James Cameron (D) Linda Hamilton, Edward Furlong, Robert Patrick, Joe Morton.

BUSY ISLAND
TASK FORCE
USS ENTERPRISE

INDEX

Numbers in *italics* indicate illustrations